TURNING POINTS

By Donna Reynolds

THE CIVIL WAR

Cavendish Square
New York

Published in 2021 by Cavendish Square Publishing, LLC 243 5th Avenue, Suite 136, New York, NY 10016

First Edition

Portions of this work were originally authored by Don Nardo and published as *The Civil War* (*American History*). All new material this edition authored by Donna Reynolds.

All websites were available and accurate when this book was sent to press.

Library of Congress Cataloging-in-Publication Data

Names: Reynolds, Donna, author.
Title: The Civil War / Donna Reynolds.
Description: First edition. | New York : Cavendish Square Publishing, [2021] | Series: Turning points | Includes bibliographical references and index.
Identifiers: LCCN 2019050820 (print) | LCCN 2019050821 (ebook) | ISBN 9781502657633 (library binding) | ISBN 9781502657626 (paperback) | ISBN 9781502657640 (ebook)
Subjects: LCSH: United States–History–Civil War, 1861-1865–Juvenile literature.
Classification: LCC E468 .R468 2021 (print) | LCC E468 (ebook) | DDC 973.7–dc23
LC record available at https://lccn.loc.gov/2019050820
LC ebook record available at https://lccn.loc.gov/2019050821

Editor: Jennifer Lombardo
Copy Editor: Michelle Denton
Designer: Deanna Paternostro

CPSIA compliance information: Batch #CS20CSQ: For further information contact Cavendish Square Publishing LLC, New York, New York, at 1-877-980-4450.

Printed in the United States of America

TABLE OF CONTENTS

INTRODUCTION

A NATION DIVIDED

A civil war is any war that is fought among the citizens of the same country. It is not the same as a revolution or rebellion, which is when the citizens of a country fight their leaders in order to establish a new system of government; however, a revolution often pits citizens against each other, as some may not support the rebels' cause. "Civil war" has also been used as a term to describe any major conflict within one group—not necessarily a country. One example of this in media is the 2016 Marvel movie *Captain America: Civil War*, in which the members of the Avengers fight each other because they have different opinions about what actions the team should take.

Civil wars have been common throughout history and around the world: The Roman Empire, Norway, Denmark, England, Japan, Russia, Australia, Argentina, Greece, Nigeria, Sri Lanka, and Syria are just a few of the many countries that have experienced such a war. The American Civil War, which took place from 1861 to 1865, is, therefore, not unique to world history. However, it is an important part of American history that has shaped the way the country operates today.

More Americans died in the Civil War than have died in any other war. According to historian J. David Hacker, about

This photograph of soldiers' graves was taken in 1865, the year the American Civil War ended.

750,000 people died in this war. Based on the population of the country at the time, this means one out of every ten white men of age to serve in the military died in the Civil War.

The number of casualties reflects only part of the great human cost of the war. Consider that those who died were brothers, fathers, sons, grandchildren, friends, and more to countless others who survived the battles or who were left on the home front. After the war ended, a huge fraction of the population was not there to help the nation piece itself back together.

This turning point in American history fundamentally changed the young nation. David Blight, a Civil War historian at Yale University, explained, "The Civil War left a culture of death, a culture of mourning, beyond anything Americans had ever experienced or imagined … It left a degree of family and social devastation unprecedented for any Western society."[1]

Keeping a Record

The American Civil War was also unique because it was one of the most extensively documented wars in history. The surviving evidence includes many thousands of letters, diaries, reports by journalists, political speeches, memoirs written after the war's end, sketches by newspaper artists, photos, maps made by military personnel, and relics such as flags, uniforms, and weapons.

Speeches from the Civil War era provide a clear picture of the sharp political differences of opinion between North and South that ultimately drove them to violence. Speeches also document the social, legal, and moral beliefs of the opposing combatants. Some of these speeches have become famous and are frequently quoted. Particularly memorable are several speeches delivered by Abraham Lincoln. As US president during the war, Lincoln succeeded in preventing the nation's permanent breakup. His Gettysburg Address in 1863 and Second Inaugural Address in 1865 are recognized by many to be among history's noblest democratic statements.

Many other speeches from that period, though less well known, are no less revealing. Jefferson Davis's inaugural address, delivered in February 1861, is one example. As the newly elected president of the Confederate States of America—often simply called the Confederacy—Davis outlined the South's reasons for departing from the Union. The Southern states had a right to secede, or break away, he stated, for the same reason that Britain's 13 American colonies had a right to revolt against British oppression during the American Revolution. He cited the American ideal "that government rests upon the consent of the governed, and that it is the right of the people to alter or abolish a government whenever it becomes destructive of the ends for which it was established."[2] Many Southerners believed the US government was becoming destructive by infringing on their right to own slaves. Lincoln and other Northerners rejected this argument; they felt that all states were subject to the laws of the federal government and that states could not simply secede whenever they did not agree with a particular law. This was the heart of the conflict between the North and the South.

CHAPTER ONE

HEADING TOWARD CONFLICT

The issue of slavery had been debated long before the beginning of the Civil War. Tensions surrounding this issue had been steadily rising, but the country had always been able to avoid outright war through a series of compromises. For example, when the US Constitution was written, Southern states wanted their slaves to count toward their population so they would have greater representation in Congress. Northern states opposed this, arguing that in all other respects, people viewed their slaves as property. Eventually, the framers of the Constitution agreed on the Three-Fifths Compromise, in which each slave counted as three-fifths of a person for Congressional representation.

This compromise led to others as the United States tried to maintain a power balance between the North and the South. For example, the Missouri Compromise of 1820 set up a system where new states would be admitted to the Union two at a time; one would be a free state, and the other would be a slave state. It also specified the exact point at which slavery became illegal: 36 degrees, 30 minutes north latitude. Above that line, slavery would be outlawed in any new states; below it, it would be actively encouraged.

The Southern economy relied heavily on cotton. The cotton gin (*left*), invented in 1794, could quickly and easily separate cotton from its seeds. However, the efficiency of this new process increased the demand for cotton and, in turn, for slaves to pick it.

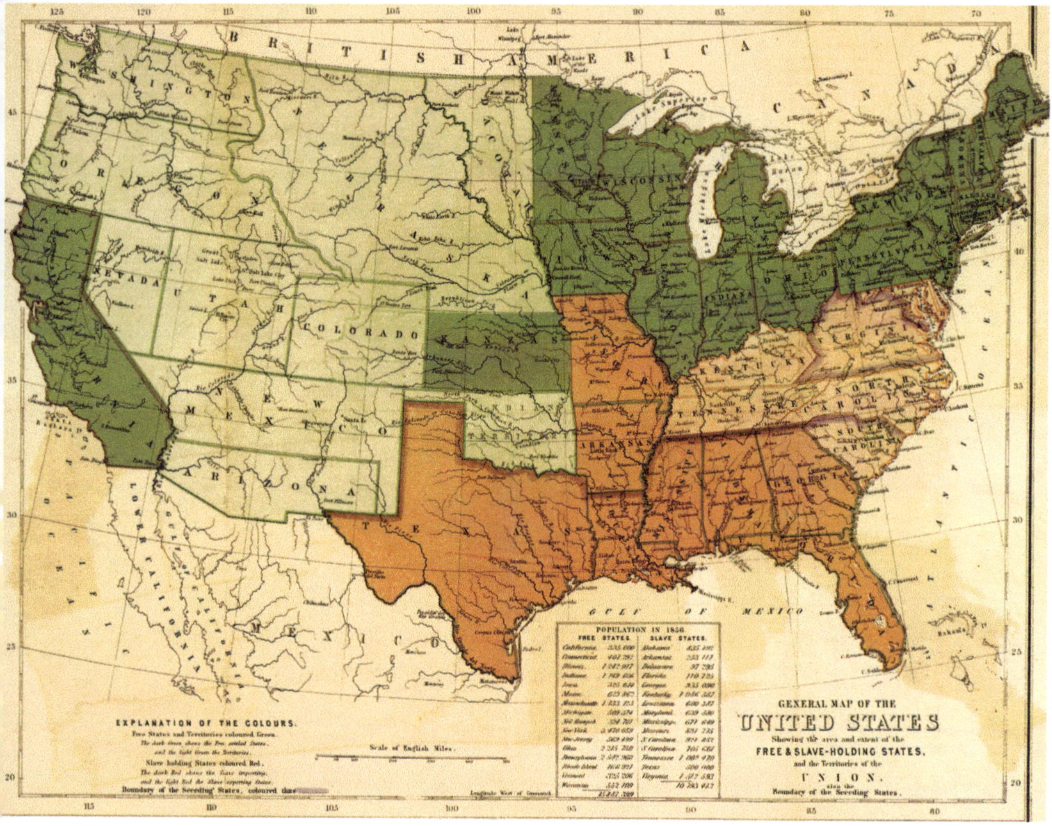

This is a map of the United States from around the time of the Civil War. The green states on this map were free states, and the orange ones were slave states.

By the beginning of the war, the North included Illinois, Ohio, Michigan, and the other states bordering the Great Lakes, Pennsylvania, New York, and the New England states. The South encompassed Virginia, Tennessee, North Carolina, South Carolina, and the states lying to their south, plus Arkansas, Louisiana, and Texas. These two regions had developed marked differences in economies, especially as the Industrial Revolution took hold in the North. The South defended its use of slavery to drive its plantation-based economy, while Northern abolitionists condemned slavery's immorality.

Different Economies

How had the residents of the South and their fellow citizens in the North come to inhabit what were essentially two distinct societies? First, there were glaring inequalities between where the two groups lived and how they made their money. The North had become highly urbanized in the 19th century's first half; 25 percent of Northerners lived in cities in 1860. The North had also become highly industrialized since 1800. It had about 1.3 million factory workers in 1860—compared to only 110,000 in the South—and 90 percent of all US manufactured goods were produced in the North. A great deal of resentment developed in the South over this Northern economic advantage.

In contrast, at the same point in time, at least 90 percent of Southerners lived in rural areas. The vast majority of people in the South—80 percent—made their living in agriculture, compared to only 40 percent in the North. Most Southerners were either poor or lower-middle class. Meanwhile, a small number of rich Southern plantation owners benefited hugely from the profits of Southern agriculture. Their main crop was cotton, which accounted for 57 percent of all US foreign exports. The cotton-producing plantation system was where the South's economic power came from. South Carolinian James Hammond exaggerated only a little when he said in 1858, "No power on earth dares … to make war on cotton. Cotton is king."[1] However, picking cotton was backbreaking work, so to ensure that they had a steady supply of reliable workers, plantation owners used slaves.

Many Southerners saw themselves as dependent on—and at the mercy of—the manufacturing economy of the North. However, modern-day economists have suggested that this was due in large part to the fact that the South's economy relied on slavery. It seems like common sense that owning a slave would cost less money than hiring a worker who would need to be paid, but in reality, according to historian Eugene Genovese, "the antebellum [pre-Civil War] South was not profit-seeking. In fact, slavery was not even meant to be profitable. Slaveowners were keener on flaunting their vast plantations and huge reserves of slaves than they were about profits and investment … Economies which used slavery may, in the long run, have been at a disadvantage."[2] Other economists have made similar suggestions. Ralph Anderson and Robert Gallman pointed out that, in order to be able to afford to feed, house, and clothe many slaves, plantation owners had to do more than grow only one crop in case that crop failed. However, this made it hard for the South to develop a manufacturing industry. Therefore, the very thing Southerners resented about the North could likely have been resolved by freeing their slaves.

The North and South also differed in their degrees of educational and technological progress. Nearly half of all Southerners, including most slaves, were illiterate in the 1850s, compared to only 6 percent of Northerners. About twice as many young Northerners attended school as young Southerners did, and the North produced twice as many doctors, teachers, and artists and six times as many inventors and engineers as the South did.

Most Southerners did not view these differences as failings or disadvantages, however. Southern lawyer and planter George Fitzhugh spoke for a majority of his neighbors when he wrote in 1854:

> *At the slaveholding South, all is at peace, quiet, plenty, and contentment. We have no mobs, no trade unions, no strikes for higher wages … [We have a] feeling of independence and equality [among whites] that distinguishes us; hence that pride of character, that self-respect, that give us ascendancy when we come into contact with Northerners. It is a distinction to be a Southerner.*[3]

The common view of Southerners by Northerners was no less self-righteous and insulting. After touring the South in the 1850s, Northern landscape architect Frederick Law Olmsted asserted that the typical Southerner "has much less curiosity than the northerner … less inventive talent, less patient and persevering energy. And I think this … to be mainly the result of habitually leaving [a large portion of his work] to his slaves."[4]

Defending Slavery

The lack of respect Southerners and Northerners had for each other was part of the foundation of the war. They were uninterested in working toward a solution with people they viewed as inferior to them, so the issue of slavery became a wedge that was

PAST MEETS PRESENT: SLAVERY OR STATES' RIGHTS?

From the beginning of the conflict, people have disagreed about the reason why the Civil War was fought. Confederate supporters insisted it was about states' rights, while Union supporters said it was about the South's refusal to abolish slavery. This disagreement persists today. In a 2011 poll, the Pew Research Center found that 48 percent of Americans believe the war was mainly about states' rights, and 38 percent believe it was mainly about slavery. The remaining 14 percent responded either that both issues were main causes or that they were unsure of the main cause.

All the states that seceded issued a list of demands or resolutions that explained why they were choosing to secede. Furthermore, four states—Texas, Mississippi, Georgia, and South Carolina—issued documents called the Declarations of Causes. All Confederate states clearly outlined the continuation of slavery as a motivation for joining the Confederacy, and each registered their opposition to Abraham Lincoln's abolitionist tendencies. They also frequently mentioned states' rights, but in the context of the states' rights to enforce slavery as well as the right to leave the Union if they felt the federal government's actions were negatively impacting their state. The Declarations of Causes all argued that the North's failure to strictly enforce the Fugitive Slave Act of 1850—a law requiring slaves who had escaped to the North to be returned to their masters in the South if they were caught—was negatively impacting Southern states and gave them the legal right to secede. As historian John Coski summed up in an article on the American Civil War Museum's website, "The South's defense of the very real institution of slavery and of the economy, society, culture, and civilization built upon slavery was the indispensable factor that led to war."[1]

1. John Coski, "Myths & Misunderstandings: What Caused the Civil War," American Civil War Museum, accessed October 29, 2019, acwm.org/blog/myths-misunderstandings-what-caused-civil-war.

steadily driving the North and South apart. The consensus of modern historians is that slavery was the chief cause of the Civil War. The numerous cultural and economic differences between Northerners and Southerners had created an atmosphere of distrust and hostility, but these factors alone would probably not have led to all-out war. It was the right to own slaves that Southerners were willing to fight for.

Southern whites strongly defended slavery in part because by the 1850s, what they called their "peculiar institution" was deeply entrenched. There were about 3.5 million black slaves in the South. Although only about one in four families owned slaves, most of their non-slave-owning neighbors benefited indirectly from slave labor.

Indeed, cotton production had become highly dependent on slave labor. Between 1820 and 1850, Southern cotton production and profits had increased an incredible sixfold. The South's economy rested in large part on maintaining—and if possible, expanding—the cotton industry. Fully aware of this reality, wealthy slaveholders persuaded Southerners who did not have slaves that freeing the slaves would cause economic ruin and race wars in the South.

Southerners also frequently claimed that slave owners were doing black people a favor by keeping them enslaved. Without white support, the argument went, black people would lead lives of crime and despair. "The Negro, when a 'slave' to a Caucasian, is vastly higher in the scale of humanity, than when in his native state,"[5] Southerner Charles C. Burr stated. According to this view, slave owners "rescued" black people from a primitive state and gave them food, clothes, and lifelong security; slaves were essentially seen as white Southerners' pets. Not only was this dehumanizing, it also ignored the brutal treatment slaves received. This included physical and sexual abuse as well as being separated from their loved ones and being ordered to perform backbreaking labor that no white people wanted to do.

Most Southerners had so thoroughly convinced themselves that slavery was not only acceptable but also desirable, both for them and for their slaves, that they passionately rejected calls from Northerners who wanted to see the slaves freed and given rights equal

Most slaves led hard lives full of difficult manual labor, but even those who were relatively well-treated wanted to be free.

to those of whites. The position of slaveholders and most other Southerners—as well as a fair number of Northerners—was neatly, if heartlessly, summed up by Illinois politician Stephen A. Douglas. In one of his renowned 1858 debates with Abraham Lincoln during their contest for a US Senate seat, Douglas said, "I believe that this government of ours was founded, and wisely founded, upon the white basis … It was made by white men for the benefit of white men and their posterity, to be executed and managed by white men."[6]

Opposing Slavery

A growing number of people in the North passionately disagreed with the Southern rationales for slavery. Abolitionism, the movement dedicated to ending slavery, had begun in Britain and spread to the Americas in the 1700s. The abolitionists had first focused their attention on ending the Atlantic slave trade, in which millions

THEY MADE HISTORY: ABRAHAM LINCOLN

Abraham Lincoln was not an abolitionist as a young man, and as late as 1858 he still did not see abolishing slavery as a realistic option. In a debate with fellow politician Stephen A. Douglas, Lincoln said, "I am not, nor ever have been in favor of bringing about in any way the social and political equality of the white and black races, [nor] making voters or jurors of negroes, nor of qualifying them to hold office, nor to intermarry with white people."[1] Lincoln's opinion on this issue changed over time, but he never truly saw black people as equals. He eventually declared freedom for the slaves that lived in the South, but this was mainly a way to strike a blow against the South during the Civil War, not because he had come to believe in racial equality. This is clear from the fact that the Emancipation Proclamation did not apply to states that were loyal to the Union. Even after he took this action, he did not expect black and white people to live in harmony together; in fact, his first suggestion was to send all the freed slaves to a colony in Africa. When this idea was met with anger by black and white abolitionists, who pointed out that most of the black people living in the United States at that time had been born in America, Lincoln changed his mind.

1. Quoted in "Mr. Lincoln and Negro Equality," *New York Times*, December 28, 1860, www.nytimes.com/1860/12/28/archives/mr-lincoln-and-negro-equality.html.

of Africans had been shipped to the Americas and other parts of the world. Britain banned the trade in 1807; the United States did the same the following year.

However, slaveholding remained legal and continued to grow in America. By that time, enough slaves had been brought to the country that slavery could continue just by forcing slaves to have more children, who would also be slaves. For this reason, abolitionists worked to end slavery itself. Their efforts were significantly aided by a Protestant evangelical revival that swept through New England, New York, and other parts of the North in the first third of the 19th century. To the deeply spiritual people in this movement, slavery was a sin because they believed all people were equal in God's eyes, regardless of their skin color.

An Ongoing Fight

These and other arguments for and against slavery continued for decades. What finally brought them to a head was an increasing effort by Southerners to further expand the institution. In the 1850s, for instance, some slave owners began lobbying their legislators to reopen the slave trade. One Southerner, William L. Yancey, asked, "If it is all right to buy slaves in Virginia and carry them to New Orleans, why is it not right to buy them in Africa and carry them there?"[7]

Even more worrisome to abolitionists were increasing attempts to export slavery into the country's western territories as well as newly created states. Even Northerners who did not think slavery was a moral issue were generally against this trend for economic reasons; for example, factory owners and workers did not want to compete with unpaid labor in these areas. In August 1846, when the United States was at war with Mexico, the US House of Representatives passed the Wilmot Proviso. This law banned the importation of slavery into California, New Mexico, and other territories Americans hoped to win from Mexico. To the relief of many Southerners, Southern legislators managed to kill the bill in the Senate. Several years later, in 1850, Southerners also benefited from the Fugitive Slave Law. This controversial legislation allowed federal agents to go anywhere—including Northern states—to arrest runaway slaves and return them to their Southern owners. However, the North rarely enforced this law—something that ended up playing a large part in Southern states' desire to secede from a government they felt was not looking out for their interests.

These Southern victories were countered to some degree by the publication of *Uncle Tom's Cabin* in 1852. Written by Harriet Beecher Stowe, the daughter and wife of Northern clergymen, the novel tells the fictional story of Tom—a kind, devoutly Christian slave who is brutally beaten to death by his vicious master—and a female slave named Eliza, who escapes her master and takes refuge in Canada. The book was a huge bestseller, second only to the Bible in the 19th century, and it helped spread and intensify the abolitionist movement. Unsurprisingly, most Southerners hated Stowe and her book.

Another Southern victory occurred with the passage of the 1854 Kansas-Nebraska Act, which allowed slavery to be decided by popular sovereignty in the newly formed Kansas Territory. Almost immediately, fighting erupted there between anti- and proslavery forces in the territory; slavery supporters sacked the antislavery town of Lawrence in May 1856, provoking outrage throughout the North. These violent confrontations, which continued until Kansas was admitted to the Union as a free state in 1861, were later given the name Bleeding Kansas.

The proslavery cause scored another success in the 1857 Dred Scott court case. Scott was a slave from Missouri, where slavery was legal. His owner took him to live in Illinois, where slavery was banned, and after the owner died, Scott sued for his freedom because he had been living in a free state. The case went to the Supreme Court, which was dominated by Southerners at the time. It ruled against Scott: He was not free, the court said. Furthermore black people were not citizens, and furthermore, Congress had no right to exclude slavery from land owned by the United States.

No More Compromises

Although most Northerners strongly disapproved of the expansion of slavery into western territories, many were not sure what to do

Uncle Tom's Cabin, written by Harriet Beecher Stowe (*shown here*), fanned the flames of the abolitionist movement.

about slavery itself. They agreed that the institution was a bad thing but accepted its existence as somehow unavoidable. Most believed black people should be free but still believed they were inferior to white people. For this reason, it was unthinkable to many that black people should be given the same rights and privileges as white people, and they did not know what else could be done; if black people were not slaves but were also not allowed to own property or work alongside white people, how were they going to support themselves? This indecision kept the abolitionist movement from completing its goal but did not stop people from continuing to argue that slavery should be abolished.

Abraham Lincoln was one of the people who did not advocate freeing the slaves, but by 1858 he also strongly felt that the expansion of slavery had become dangerous to American unity. In accepting the Republican nomination for the Senate in June of that year, he made the now-famous statement:

> *"A house divided against itself cannot stand." I believe this government cannot endure, permanently half slave and half free … It will become all one thing or all the other. Either the opponents of slavery, will arrest the further spread of it … or its advocates will push it forward, till it shall become alike lawful in all the States.*[8]

However, not all abolitionists were so paralyzed by indecision. One fanatical abolitionist in his 50s, John Brown, traveled to Kansas in 1855 to help local antislavery forces fight their opponents. "[Talk] will never free the slaves," he told his followers. "What is needed is action—action."[9]

True to these words, Brown soon hatched a daring scheme that he believed would free all the slaves. He would lead a raid on the federal armory at Harpers Ferry, Virginia (now West Virginia). With the weapons taken, he would arm a group of Virginian slaves, and they would free the rest of Virginia's slaves. Then, heading southward, they would free slaves all across the South, causing its economy to collapse.

HISTORY HAPPENED HERE: HARPERS FERRY

Today, Harpers Ferry has been designated a National Historical Park and is under the care of the National Park Service. Visitors can hike, attend presentations by archaeologists, and see the many museums and exhibits the town offers. Many also enjoy the beautiful views of the Potomac and Shenandoah Rivers as well as shopping in the town, which has maintained its historical feel. Key sites in John Brown's raid are highlighted, but since the event covered several hundred miles, a complete tour of his path is impossible to lay out effectively.

In 1859, the town of Harpers Ferry, Virginia, was the site of an abolitionist raid that fueled talk of secession in the South. Today, it is a tourist attraction in West Virginia—a state that was formed after the raid—that showcases the town's role in the Civil War.

The raid occurred on October 16, 1859. Brown and 18 accomplices, including three of his sons, succeeded in capturing the armory. However, the authorities were alerted, and

FROM THE SOURCE: JOHN BROWN'S SPEECH

Before the sentencing at his trial, John Brown gave an eloquent speech that included these words:

> *I deny everything but what I have all along admitted: of a design on my part to free slaves ... This court acknowledges ... I suppose, the validity of the law of God. I see a book kissed, which I suppose to be the Bible, or at least the New Testament, which teaches me that all things whatsoever I would that men should do to me, I should do even so to them ... Now, if it is deemed necessary that I should forfeit my life for the furtherance of the ends of justice, and mingle my blood further with the blood of my children and with the blood of millions in this slave country whose rights are disregarded by wicked, cruel, and unjust enactments, I say, let it be done.*[1]

1. Quoted in Oswald G. Villard, *John Brown, 1800–1859: A Biography Fifty Years After* (Boston, MA: Houghton Mifflin, 1911), pp. 498–99.

some local militiamen cornered and killed some of the raiders. On the morning of October 18, government troops arrived and arrested Brown and his surviving followers. After a trial, he was hanged on December 2, 1859.

News of the Harpers Ferry raid shocked and enraged people across the South. At first, many Southerners believed wild rumors claiming that an army of abolitionists and rebellious slaves was invading the Southern states. Even after it became obvious that these rumors were false, they further inflamed widespread hatred and distrust of Northern "Yankees," and many Southerners began openly talking about seceding from the Union.

In the North, meanwhile, Brown was widely seen as a hero and martyr to the cause of human freedom. Increasing numbers of Americans believed Brown's use of violence was the only way slavery could be abolished, which did not bode well for the nation's future.

How You See History

1. Why do you think people would want to own slaves if it was costing them more money than it was saving them?
2. Do you think the Civil War was mainly about states' rights or about slavery? Explain your answer.
3. Do you agree with John Brown's actions? Why or why not?

CHAPTER TWO

A NATION AT WAR

Although John Brown was one of the only people to use violence to try to accomplish abolition, many Northerners shared his feeling that some kind of action needed to be taken. In response, Southerners spread rumors that everyone in the North was violent and unable to be reasoned with. The issue also had huge implications for politics. Suspicion and hostility toward the Republican Party grew as Democrats tried to draw parallels between the Republican antislavery platform and Brown's raid. Democrats wanted voters to believe that Republicans thought violence was the solution to the problem of slavery, even though most actually condemned Brown's actions. Republicans, including soon-to-be presidential nominee Abraham Lincoln, publicly distanced themselves from Brown, but many in the South would view the election of Lincoln as a reason for secession.

Talk of secession—of ending the "union" between North and South—was loudest in South Carolina, but it soon spread to other Southern states. Heated debate grew about whether secession was legal under the Constitution. Nowhere in the Constitution did it say that states could not secede. Pro-secessionists asserted that states still maintained such powers over the federal government. Some

Charles Sumner was admired in his home state of Massachusetts for his abolitionist work, which played a part in the events that led to war. This statue of Sumner, which was designed by sculptor Anne Whitney after the senator's death in 1874, sits in Harvard Square in Cambridge, Massachusetts.

believed that whether or not it was legal, the Southern states should leave the Union the same way the American colonies had left Great Britain. Southerners who felt this way used phrases similar to those spoken about the American Revolution. A Confederate army officer later recalled, "I took up arms … upon a broader ground—the right of revolution. We were wronged. Our properties and liberties were about to be taken from us. It was a sacred duty to rebel."[1]

Lincoln and others took the position that secession was illegal. Allowing it would set a dangerous precedent, or example for future situations, and cause the United States to fall into chaos. Lincoln believed that if he allowed the South to secede, other states would be able to leave when they wanted for any reason.

Sumner's Caning

Senator Charles Sumner of Massachusetts had long felt disdain for Southerners. Those feelings turned into outright hatred after a famous episode that occurred in 1856. On May 19 and 20, Sumner delivered a speech in the Senate in which he harshly condemned the proslavery activities in Kansas. He also verbally attacked Andrew Butler of South Carolina, a coauthor of the Kansas-Nebraska Act. Two days later, Preston Brooks, a US congressman and close relative of Butler's, went to the Senate chamber. Finding Sumner sitting at his desk, he beat him over the head at least 30 times with a wooden cane, then left him, bleeding and unconscious, on the floor.

In the North, people were furious over the attack. "Are we to be chastised [punished] as they [Southerners] chastise their slaves?" asked an editor of the *New York Evening Post*. "Are we, too, slaves [and] a target of their brutal blows, when we do not comport [behave] ourselves to please them?"[2] In the South, though, Brooks was a hero. "The vulgar abolitionists in the Senate are getting above themselves," the *Richmond Enquirer* stated. "They must be lashed into submission."[3] The assault on Sumner exemplified the extreme tensions, intolerance, and hatred that had built up between Southerners and Northerners. However, Sumner's caning did not stop him. After a three-year absence spent recovering from his wounds, Sumner returned to the Senate and resumed his verbal attacks on slavery, once more angering his Southern colleagues.

FROM THE SOURCE: "ON THE CRIME AGAINST KANSAS"

In May 1856, Charles Sumner delivered his now-famous speech, "On the Crime Against Kansas." In this excerpt from his speech, he discusses what he believed to be the motives behind the attempts to introduce slavery into the territory of Kansas, which he saw as a way for those who supported slavery to continue to gain political power through the introduction of new slave states:

> *The wickedness which I now begin to expose is immeasurably aggravated by the motive which prompted it ... it may be clearly traced to a depraved longing for a new slave State, the hideous offspring of such a crime, in the hope of adding to the power of slavery in the National Government. Yes, sir, when the whole world ... is rising up to condemn this wrong ... here in our Republic, force, ay, sir, FORCE has been openly employed in compelling Kansas to this pollution, and all for the sake of political power. There is the simple fact, which you will in vain attempt to deny, but which in itself presents an essential wickedness that makes other public crimes seem like public virtues.*[1]

1. Quoted in Neil Kagan and Stephen G. Hyslop, *Eyewitness to the Civil War: The Complete History from Secession to Reconstruction* (Washington, DC: National Geographic, 2006), p. 20.

Still more Southern hatred for the North was generated by Abraham Lincoln's election in the fall of 1860. Although he did not receive a single electoral vote from any Southern state, he got 59 percent of the nation's total electoral votes, which secured his victory. Most Southerners viewed his win as an utter disaster. It appeared to them that a Northern antislavery party—the recently organized

Republicans—would dominate the US government for the foreseeable future, potentially dooming the South's cherished institution of slavery. This fear caused many Southerners to make dire predictions—many of which were greatly exaggerated and turned out, in time, to be false. "Do you love your mother, your wife, your sister, your daughter?" an outraged Georgian asked his state's slave owners. In a nation "ruled by Lincoln," he said, "in ten years or less our children will be the slaves of Negroes."[4]

Opposing Secession

Many pro-secession Southerners disliked and distrusted Lincoln so much they may have wished the outgoing president, James Buchanan, could stay in office. Buchanan had endorsed the Dred Scott decision, and throughout his term, which had begun in 1857, he had sympathized with slave owners and those who wanted to expand slavery into the territories. Many people, therefore, believed he would approve of Southern secession too. However, this was not the case. In his last speech to Congress, delivered on December 3, 1860, Buchanan angered many Southerners by saying that states had no constitutional right to secede from the Union.

Numerous Northern newspapers and politicians agreed with this view. "The doctrine of secession is anarchy," a Cincinnati newspaper editorial asserted. "If any minority have the right to break up the government at pleasure … there is an end of all government."[5]

Regardless of the president's opinion, the members of South Carolina's legislature voted unanimously on December 20, 1860, to secede from the Union. Hoping to calm Southern fears and prevent further secessions, Lincoln wrote to his former congressional colleague Alexander Stephens of Georgia two days later to assure him that he had no intention of ending slavery.

This and other Northern calls for reason and moderation failed, however. By February 1, 1861, six more Southern states—Mississippi, Florida, Alabama, Georgia, Louisiana, and Texas—had seceded. A few days later, their representatives, along with those from South Carolina, came together in Montgomery, Alabama, to form the Confederate States of America. Buchanan, who was still president at

Shown here is the official flag of the Confederate States of America. The flag is sometimes called the "stars and bars," and it is much less well known than the Confederate battle flag that became the symbol of the Confederacy after the war.

the time (Lincoln did not officially take office until March 4, 1861), did nothing to stop them. In April and May, four more states—Arkansas, Tennessee, North Carolina, and Virginia—left the Union and joined the Confederacy. (In June 1863, the northwestern part of Virginia broke away and became the Union state of West Virginia.)

The Confederates' new constitution revealed that the issues foremost in their minds were slavery and states' rights. The document resembled the US Constitution in many ways, but the few differences were major ones. There was no Supreme Court in the Confederate version, for example; the powerful state legislatures were allowed to remove federal judges trying cases within their borders. The executive branch was weakened by limiting the president to a single six-year term. Most importantly, slavery was strongly protected, not only in the existing states, but also in any territories or new states that might become part of the Confederacy.

In addition to working on their new constitution, Confederate leaders hurried to secure their military power. They seized control of or claimed authority over all federal forts and navy yards within their borders. Most did not expect an immediate Northern attack, yet they did not trust Lincoln and worried that he might try to break up the Confederacy, considering how strongly he had opposed secession.

Attack on Fort Sumter

True to his word, Lincoln decided to take a cautious but firm stand against the secessionists by ordering a relief expedition to Fort Sumter. Situated on a small island at the entrance to the harbor of Charleston, South Carolina, the federal installation was an imposing building. With its 40-foot-high (12 meter) walls and large battery of cannons, it easily commanded naval commerce entering the port. The new president sent a message to local authorities in Charleston informing them that he was sending the fort food and other provisions only. "No effort to throw in men, arms, or ammunition, will be made, without further notice," he said, "or in the case of an attack upon the Fort."[6]

Nonaggressive as it supposedly was, the supply expedition to the fort gave Confederate leaders an excuse to take their own firm stand. They were under pressure from all quarters in the South to send a strong warning to Lincoln and other Northerners who might consider interfering in the affairs of the Confederate states. After meeting with his cabinet on April 9, 1861, Jefferson Davis ordered General P. G. T. Beauregard to seize Fort Sumter before the supply ships arrived.

Beauregard first went to the fort's commander, Major Robert Anderson, and demanded his surrender. When Anderson refused, Confederate guns opened fire on the fort at 4:30 a.m. on April 12, 1861. After 33 hours of almost continuous bombardment, Anderson had no choice but to surrender.

The reaction in the North to the capture of Fort Sumter was swift and almost universal outrage. The fact that Confederates had fired on the American flag inspired an intense show of patriotism in Northern states. Near Boston, Massachusetts, a Harvard University professor said that "the whole population, men, women, and children, seem to be in the streets with [US] flags."[7] The Confederates were officially seen as traitors to the United States.

HISTORY HAPPENED HERE: CHARLESTON, SOUTH CAROLINA

Charleston is a popular tourist destination that offers attractions such as art museums, a maritime museum, wildlife ocean tours, and botanical gardens. Furthermore, Charleston has embraced its rich history, offering many museums, exhibits, and tours for people who are interested in the Civil War era. For instance, people can visit Fort Sumter and tour old plantations to see how both the owners and the slaves lived.

Charleston has also made an effort to recognize and promote the unique history of black Americans. As one of the first US cities to start using African slaves, its history has been greatly influenced by their culture, including food, arts, and agricultural innovations. In turn, they were influenced by the country they were forced to live in. This combination of cultures gave rise to the Gullah—also known as Geechee—people, who have their own language, food, music, religion, and other cultural features created by combining American and African traditions. Although they have been living in the United States for centuries, it was not until 1992 that that National Park Service began highlighting Gullah culture and accomplishments. In October 2006, the Gullah Geechee Cultural Heritage Corridor was created in Charleston to showcase the Gullah people and their way of life, which is still vibrant and active today in certain parts of the United States, including South Carolina.

Lincoln, too, viewed the attack on the fort as treason and intended to respond accordingly. On April 15, he called for 75,000 volunteer soldiers to enlist for three months to put down what he now called an insurrection. Within two weeks, 35,000 of these troops had arrived in Washington, DC.

This picture illustrates the bombardment of Fort Sumter in 1861.

The president's primary aim throughout the entire conflict was to preserve the Union. Shortly after the fall of Fort Sumter, he said, "We must settle this question now, whether in a free government the minority have the right to break up the government whenever they choose. If we fail it will go far to prove the incapability of the people to govern themselves."[8] Lincoln's intentions were good, but the idea that he would need only 75,000 troops for three months was a major miscalculation.

Ready for War

After Fort Sumter, a real battle between the states was inevitable, as was loss of life. It is important to remember that the terms "North" and "South" give only a general idea of the opposing sides. In reality, loyalties were not so clear-cut.

Not all slave-holding states joined the Confederacy, but that did not mean the people who lived there were firmly pro-Union. The state governments decided whether to stay or leave the Union, but many private citizens held their own views. For example, more than 46,000 soldiers from Maryland fought for the Union, while about 25,000 Marylanders joined the Confederate army.

Families, like states, were fractured over the war. For instance, the Shriver brothers of Maryland lived on the same homestead, separated by a road. Andrew Shriver owned household slaves, but he sided with the Union. William Shriver, who owned no slaves, supported the Confederacy. Both sent sons to join the armies of the North and South. This is only one of hundreds of examples of family members joining opposite sides. In all, about 100,000 men from Northern border states fought for the South. About 45,000 white Southern men fought for the Union, along with at least that many former Southern slaves.

At the beginning of the war, each side had great hope of a quick and decisive victory, fueled by a sense of righteousness. The country had experienced a relatively short conflict in the Mexican-American War, which was fought between 1846 and 1848. Many expected an even briefer conflict, perhaps a few battles and the capture of the enemy capital. Many Northerners thought the South would merely give up after the first battle. Some Southerners held a view of Northerners as cowardly and ill-prepared soldiers.

Another naïve belief was that the war would not affect civilians; many people assumed battles would be fought in open and remote areas. Each side eventually learned the hard way that the conflict would be far longer and deadlier than anyone had predicted.

Creating Strategies

The initial unrealistic outlook about the war made it seem unnecessary to adopt the kind of strategy needed to fight a long conflict. In the North, for example, the general view was that it would not be necessary to conquer the entire South. Instead, Northerners thought their army would defeat the Southern rebels, arrest their leaders, and quickly regain the loyalty of the general population.

Winfield Scott, the Union's chief general at the time, disagreed. He foresaw a more orderly, time-consuming approach in which Northern forces would steadily surround the South and force it into submission by cutting off its commerce and supplies, like a snake squeezing the life out of its victim. However, he knew most Northerners would not support this kind of drawn-out conflict. Indeed, Northern public opinion demanded a quick strike against Confederate forces in northern Virginia. Like Scott, Lincoln was wary of rushing in but thought that such a strike was worth a try.

In contrast, the South's initial strategy was to maintain its independence by defending its land and water borders. These stretched more than 6,000 miles (9,660 kilometers) and covered about 750,000 square miles (1.9 million sq km) of territory. The early Southern military strategy called for defending its borders and attacking into the North. For this reason, Southern generals often called it an "offensive-defensive" approach. On the defensive side, small or moderate-size armies would move to various points near the borders to halt invasions by Northern armies. A disadvantage of this approach was that it left gaps in the defenses that the North might easily penetrate, but this shortcoming was partly offset by the

Winfield Scott originally wanted to take a slow and steady approach to the Civil War, but public opinion prevented him from doing so.

strategy's offensive aspect: Confederate armies would sometimes go on the attack and hope to score major victories, thereby damaging Northern morale and swiftly ending the war.

This Southern strategy stemmed partly from a feeling of superiority in the South. It was a common belief at the time that the average Southern man was more civilized and braver than any Northerner, making it easy for the Southern soldiers to defeat the Northern ones. Another reason the offensive-defensive strategy was adopted was the unusual amount of power and autonomy the Confederate Constitution gave to individual states. Instead of having a unified army directed by a central government, individual states could choose where to send—or not send—their soldiers. Historian James M. McPherson explained, "The governors of, say, South Carolina and Arkansas were unwilling to send most of their regiments to crucial points in Virginia and Tennessee if this would leave their own states unprotected."[9]

Battles at Sea and on Land

In the war's first year, both the North and South had limited military strategies and goals and hoped to end the war quickly and with minimal losses. Neither side was operating at full capacity yet, so they each initially experienced some degree of success along with some major setbacks.

For the North, the biggest success in this period was its naval blockade of the South. In April 1861, Lincoln ordered the Union navy to seal off all major Southern ports. The aim was to keep the South from exporting cotton and other goods to foreign nations. This would hurt the South's economy and prevent other nations from shipping supplies into the Confederacy.

Despite these sanctions, many ships did try to evade the blockade, and some of these "blockade runners" were successful. However, these efforts made only a small dent in the blockade. Thus, Southern leaders felt that they needed to find a way to destroy or scare away the Northern ships and gain control of the seas.

To achieve this goal, Confederate naval secretary Stephen Mallory worked to construct the first operational all-metal warship, called an ironclad. Early in March 1862, the *Virginia* (originally a wooden ship called the *Merrimack*) was ready to prove itself. It was 270 feet (82 m) long, sported 800 tons (726 metric tons) of iron plates, a huge iron ram in its bow, and 10 powerful cannons. The *Virginia* attacked and sank a Union warship, the USS *Cumberland*, at Hampton Roads, Virginia, and badly damaged two other enemy ships.

On March 8, seemingly out of nowhere, the first Union ironclad, the *Monitor*, appeared on the scene, and the two metal monsters engaged in furious combat. In the historic battle, the smaller *Monitor* consistently outmaneuvered the *Virginia*, but neither vessel managed to score a clear-cut victory. For the South, this standoff was no better than a loss. It invalidated the Confederacy's attempt to achieve naval equality with the North, and the blockade remained in effect.

The South originally did much better on land. Its first major military success was its stunning victory in the First Battle of Bull Run, also called the Battle of First Manassas. (Bull Run was the name of a local stream, and Manassas was a nearby railroad station.) The new Confederate government decided to switch its capital from Montgomery, Alabama, to Richmond, Virginia, in early summer 1861. Immediately, Northern legislators began demanding that Lincoln and his generals capture Richmond as quickly as possible—a demand backed up by public opinion. To accomplish this plan, Union commander Major General Irvin McDowell needed to push aside General P. G. T. Beauregard's army, which was stationed at Manassas Junction, Virginia, about 25 miles (40 km) from Washington, DC.

On July 21, 1861, McDowell and his federal troops approached Bull Run Creek near Manassas. Behind the army were thousands of civilians, some carrying picnic baskets, who expected to witness a short and decisive Union victory. For a while, many of the Confederates did retreat. However, confusion and delays in the Union ranks and the arrival of Southern reinforcements allowed the Confederates to counterattack, and soon the Northern troops were forced to completely retreat. The death toll at Bull Run was relatively small—418 Union soldiers and 387 Confederates—but more than 1,000 soldiers in each army were wounded. The First Battle of Bull

This 1862 picture shows the *Monitor* (*front left*) and the *Virginia* (*middle*) firing at each other.

Run worried people on both sides by demonstrating that the conflict was goin[illegible] neither short nor easy.

Fighting in [illegible] East

In the wake of McDowell's embarrassing loss at Bull Run, Lincoln replaced him, giving charge of the Union Army of the Potomac to Major General George B. McClellan. That same day, McClellan wrote to his wife, Ellen, to tell her that he was confident he could come up with a better strategy and lead the Union to victory.

McClellan's hopes and predictions of success proved premature, however. Early in 1862, he led his army in a major thrust into northeastern Virginia, which became known as the Peninsular Campaign. It was one of many campaigns and battles that took place in the war's principal region of conflict, which became known as the Eastern Theater; it consisted mainly of Virginia, Maryland, the District of Columbia, Pennsylvania, and eastern North Carolina. McClellan tried to move on Richmond, but he took heavy losses in the Battle of Seven Pines on May 31 and June 1, 1862, as well as the Seven Days Battles (six battles fought between June 25 and July 1 in the Richmond area). In those six battles, Confederate military leader Robert E. Lee, aided by his subordinate generals, James Longstreet and Thomas "Stonewall" Jackson, drove McClellan away from Richmond and into full retreat.

Lee followed up on his victories by marching his army northward toward Washington, DC. Between August 28 and 30, Lee's army met the Union's newly formed Army of Virginia, under Major General John Pope, at Manassas. In what became known as the Second Battle of Bull Run (or Second Manassas), the Confederates decisively defeated Pope's forces.

A few days later, Lee led about 45,000 troops across the Potomac River into Northern territory. On September 17, 1862, the Confederates met their greatest test yet near Antietam Creek, outside of Sharpsburg, Maryland. The Union forces were commanded by McClellan, aided by Major General Ambrose Burnside, Major General Joseph Hooker, and other key officers. As had happened at the First Battle of Bull Run, thousands of civilians gathered to watch.

It turned out to be a show that most of the onlookers wished they had not seen. More Americans were killed or wounded in the Battle of Antietam (or Sharpsburg) than on any other day in the country's history before or since. The staggering casualty figures were 3,654 killed, 17,292 wounded, and 1,771 missing (many of whom likely died).

Although both sides suffered badly in the fight, it was seen as a Union victory because Lee had to retreat over the Potomac into Virginia. McClellan had technically won the battle, but because he failed to pursue the Confederates and deal them a knockout blow, Lincoln replaced him with Burnside on November 7, 1862.

Burnside did no better, however. When he attempted to capture Richmond in mid-December, he was disastrously defeated by Lee near Fredericksburg, Virginia. Several failed frontal charges by Burnside's troops resulted in terrible Union losses. Afterward, the frustrated Lincoln fired Burnside and appointed Joseph Hooker in his place. Hooker, too, failed to overcome Lee. Though his forces outnumbered Lee's two to one, Hooker was defeated at Chancellorsville in north-central Virginia between April 30 and May 6, 1863.

The Second Battle of Bull Run (*shown here*), like the first, resulted in a Confederate victory.

Hooker lost more than 17,000 men—dead, wounded, or missing—which was around 15 percent of his forces.

Fighting in the West

The awful losses the Union had suffered in the war's Eastern Theater between July 1861 and May 1863 were disheartening to Northerners, but some hope was restored as better news periodically trickled in from the more distant Western Theater, which largely encompassed the regions lying west of the Appalachian Mountains. Historians sometimes designate the areas west of the Mississippi River separately as the Trans-Mississippi Theater.

Indeed, the Confederates were far less successful in the West throughout the war than they were in the East in the conflict's first two years. Union forces captured Tennessee's capital, Nashville, in

THEY MADE HISTORY: CLARA BARTON

Massachusetts native Clara Barton became the most famous of the many brave and selfless nurses who attended to wounded and dying men in the Civil War. One of Barton's finest and most famous moments occurred in the middle of the slaughter at Antietam in September 1862. Riding in a wagon filled with medical supplies and food, she followed the sound of the guns to a small farmhouse that was filled with wounded soldiers. As bullets rained down from all sides, she aided Union army surgeon James Dunn, whom she had met at an army hospital a few months before. For hours, she dragged incapacitated men to safety, gave them water, and bandaged their wounds. She also narrowly escaped death herself when a bullet passed through one of her sleeves. Stunned at her devotion and courage under fire, Dunn later called Barton "the true heroine of the age, the angel of the battlefield."[1]

1. Quoted in "Clara Barton," History.com, modified May 13, 2019, www.history.com/topics/womens-history/clara-barton.

Later in her life, Clara Barton helped found the American Red Cross, which provides aid in emergency situations.

February 1862. The next month, Union general Samuel R. Curtis defeated Confederate general Earl Van Dorn in the Battle of Pea Ridge in northwest Arkansas. The Union also won control of most of nearby Missouri. In April, a US naval force commanded by David G. Farragut seized control of New Orleans, Louisiana, providing the Union with access to the Mississippi River on the Confederacy's western flank.

Farther upstream in that same month, Major General Ulysses S. Grant won a narrow Union victory on land over Confederate generals P. G. T. Beauregard and Albert S. Johnston. The site of the conflict was Shiloh in southwestern Tennessee. One of the bloodiest battles ever fought on American soil, it produced a death toll of 1,754 on the Union side and 1,728 on the Confederate side. Grant went on to lay siege to Vicksburg, Mississippi, from May 18 to July 4, 1863, which allowed him to capture this important Southern city. These victories gave the Union almost complete control of the Mississippi River.

Many miles to the west, meanwhile, Union forces fought to secure control of Arizona and New Mexico. Confederate groups from Texas had invaded these areas in 1861 and established the Confederate territory of Arizona, but these occupiers were forced to withdraw when Union reinforcements arrived from southern California early in 1862. In the small but pivotal Battle of Glorieta Pass, fought on March 26, 1862, in northern New Mexico, about 1,300 Union troops defeated an equally sized enemy force, thereby keeping the Confederacy from establishing a foothold in the Rocky Mountains and the far west.

How You See History

1. Do you think the Civil War could have been avoided? If so, how?
2. Why do you think Southerners were so concerned about Lincoln even though he hadn't made freeing the slaves one of his campaign promises?
3. Why didn't the war end as quickly as people assumed it would?

CHAPTER THREE

1863: A PIVOTAL YEAR

The year 1863 turned out to be a turning point in the Civil War. Although no one knew it yet, it was the midpoint of the war; it had been going on for two years before and would continue for two more after. Up until this point, the South was still confident in its ability to win. The Confederate army had inflicted heavy casualties on the Union forces, and the Union had been forced to completely change its original strategy and settle in for a longer conflict. The North had more resources at its disposal, but the South was hoping to simply outlast the North, not overturn the federal government. Southerners hoped the North would simply get tired of fighting and give up, and they were sure they could hold out until that happened.

Defeats of the Union army, especially in the summer and autumn of 1862, were taking their toll on the North, giving rise to so-called Peace Democrats (called Copperheads by Republicans) from Midwestern states who threatened to join the Confederacy or perhaps even start their own new nation. Lincoln knew some decisive victories—confidence-building events—were needed to put an end to this kind of talk.

Three turning points in 1863 were central to accelerating the Confederacy's collapse and the end of the deep-rooted Southern way

This 1863 wood engraving shows former slaves escaping to Union territory after Lincoln announced the end of slavery in the South. Although they were technically free, escaping could still be dangerous because Southerners paid no attention to Lincoln's words.

of life. Lincoln himself had laid the groundwork for the first: the Emancipation Proclamation, which officially announced the end of slavery in the South. Though he had issued the proclamation in September 1862, it officially went into effect January 1, 1863. Still, the results were not immediate. There was no way for the federal government to enforce the proclamation in Confederate states, and naturally, Southerners did not pay attention to the command. However, slaves who heard the news escaped to the North, and black people could now fight for the Union. The Emancipation Proclamation was undeniably a giant step toward freedom for all slaves on both sides of the war.

Hurting the South

For many months, Lincoln had been thinking about issuing a proclamation freeing the Southern slaves. His primary goal was not to end slavery. Rather, he mainly hoped that freeing the slaves would inspire them to resist their masters, which would disrupt Southern society, make the war's end come faster, and thereby save the Union. "My paramount object in this struggle is to save the Union, and is not either to save or to destroy slavery," he wrote to newspaper editor Horace Greeley on August 22, 1862. He continued:

> *If I could save the Union without freeing any slave I would do it, and if I could save it by freeing all the slaves I would do it; and if I could save it by freeing some and leaving others alone I would also do that. What I do about slavery, and the colored race, I do because I believe it helps to save the Union.*[1]

Lincoln felt that the timing of the proclamation was crucial. He decided his announcement would carry more force if he issued it after a major Union victory. The Northern win at Antietam on September 17, 1862, was a narrow one, but after the long string of Union losses in the preceding months, it would have to do.

Later that day, therefore, Lincoln issued an executive order that came to be called the Emancipation Proclamation. In part, it said that on January 1, 1863, "All persons held as slaves within any State or designated part of a State, the people whereof shall then be in

PAST MEETS PRESENT:
GONE WITH THE WIND

The Civil War is a popular subject for books, movies, and TV shows. One of the most famous stories of all time is *Gone with the Wind*, a novel by Margaret Mitchell. Written in 1936 and turned into a movie three years later, *Gone with the Wind* is set before, during, and after the Civil War. It tells the story of Scarlett O'Hara, a young woman living in Georgia when the war breaks out. Throughout the war, she tries to keep her family and property safe from Union soldiers. She has several husbands, one of whom is a man named Rhett Butler. Shortly after Scarlett meets Rhett, he becomes a blockade runner, illegally bringing goods from the North into the South. After the war, Scarlett struggles to pay the high taxes the Reconstructionists pass on properties such as her family's plantation.

Gone with the Wind is not just the most popular Civil War movie, it is one of the most popular movies ever made. However, not everyone considers it a great movie. Critics say it is racist and makes slavery seem like a good thing, pointing out that in both the movie and the book, the slaves are unhappy to be freed and only wish to keep serving the O'Hara family.

rebellion against the United States, shall be then, thenceforward, and forever free."[2]

Not surprisingly, reactions to the proclamation were mixed. When January 1, the official day of freedom, came, celebrations were held in various places across the North. One took place on the Union-held Sea Islands off South Carolina's coast. There, Colonel Thomas W. Higginson, a Massachusetts clergyman who had been an abolitionist since before the war, stood before a large group of whites and blacks. Among them were the members of the First South Carolina Volunteers, the first Union regiment recruited from former black slaves, whom he had organized and trained. Higginson later recalled that when he raised the American flag so that the crowd could see it, some black people began singing "My Country 'Tis of Thee," after which most of the crowd joined in. "Firmly and irrepressibly," he wrote, "the quavering voices sang on, verse after verse … I never saw anything so electric. It made all other words cheap. It seemed the choked voice of a race at last unloosed … After it was ended, tears were everywhere."[3]

In the South, though, many whites viewed the proclamation and its consequences with fear and anger. The prospect of losing valuable property—which the slaves represented to their owners—was bad enough, but Southerners also felt their safety and superior social position were threatened. Author Rachel F. Seidman explained, "Having deluded [fooled] themselves for so long that blacks were happy as slaves and loyal and devoted to their white families, many whites were genuinely shocked and thoroughly embittered when these same slaves took the first opportunity to escape to freedom."[4]

An Epic Battle

Citizens of both the Confederacy and Union were still adjusting to the reality of Lincoln's blow against slavery when they heard the news of another turning point: the outcome of the Battle of Gettysburg, fought in July 1863. This was the war's largest and most pivotal engagement. Southern casualties were enormous, and the Confederacy never fully recovered.

The events leading up to the epic fight at Gettysburg began in mid-June 1863. In his second attempt to invade the North, General Lee moved his army into southeastern Pennsylvania. Not long afterward, Lincoln, upset over Joseph Hooker's poor performance at Chancellorsville, replaced him as leader of the Army of the Potomac with Major General George G. Meade, whose forces dealt the Confederacy a major blow at Gettysburg.

Immediately after taking command, Meade prepared for action against Lee. Both men seemed to have an initial strategy of hunkering down in a strong position and waiting for the other to attack. However, an unexpected series of events interfered. The men of one

Gettysburg National Military Park is still a popular tourist attraction for people who are interested in seeing where the Civil War was fought.

of Lee's units, commanded by Lieutenant General A. P. Hill, were in serious need of shoes, and on July 1, they went to the small town of Gettysburg to find some. There they ran into two brigades of Union cavalry led by Brigadier General John Buford. A skirmish followed. As the day progressed, it rapidly expanded as units from both armies streamed into the area as reinforcements.

During the afternoon, Lee arrived and ordered Hill and Lieutenant General Richard S. Ewell to charge the Union line, which broke and retreated to Cemetery Hill, not far south of the town. Lee saw that the hill was fortified with Union troops and cannons. He was determined to remove them and seize the high ground. However, when he told Ewell to attack, Ewell hesitated, which allowed Meade to send in more reinforcements. As the sun was setting, the Union forces set up a defensive line that stretched more than 2 miles (3.2 km) across Cemetery Hill, Culp's Hill, and Little Round Top hill.

The next day, Lee again set his sights on taking the hills. James Longstreet, who had arrived late at Gettysburg, thought it unwise

HISTORY HAPPENED HERE: GETTYSBURG, PENNSYLVANIA

The peace and beauty of modern-day Gettysburg gives no outward indication of its bloody past. However, scattered around the city and the surrounding countryside are dozens of reminders of the battle that was fought there. Visitors can take a tour of all the places where soldiers fought the three-day battle near the city. They can also witness reenactments, historical demonstrations, and museum exhibits. One of the most popular is the Jennie Wade Museum House, where Jennie Wade—the only civilian casualty of the Battle of Gettysburg—was killed. A sniper who had been practicing his marksmanship by trying to hit Wade's doorknob missed, causing the bullet to go through two doors and into Wade's back.

Due to the huge number of deaths in the battle, ghost tours are a particularly popular feature of Gettysburg. Legend has it that Wade's ghost still haunts her house, and visitors to Gettysburg have reported strange occurrences throughout the town. Ghost tours take people for a walk around town, combining information about the town's history and local legends about the spirits that haunt this infamous historical site.

to attack such a well-fortified position, but Lee could not be dissuaded. Unable to talk his commander out of attacking, Longstreet reluctantly did his duty. In some of the heaviest fighting of the war, he and his men assaulted enemy positions west of Little Round Top. However, the Confederate attacks were disjointed, whereas Meade and his officers mounted well-coordinated counterattacks. This allowed the Union army to hold its position on the hills.

On July 3—the third day of the battle—Lee remained determined to turn the tide in his favor. He ordered Longstreet to send about 14,000 troops commanded by George E. Pickett and two other officers against the strongly fortified Union center. Again, Longstreet objected, and again Lee insisted. "My heart was heavy," Longstreet later wrote. "I could see the desperate and hopeless nature of the charge and the hopeless slaughter it would cause."[5]

THEY MADE HISTORY: JAMES LONGSTREET

James Longstreet was one of the Confederacy's leading generals. Born in South Carolina in 1821, he attended West Point Military Academy, graduating in 1842 in the undesirable rank of 54th out of a class of 56 cadets. However, this did not keep him from having a celebrated military career. He served with distinction in the Mexican-American War in the late 1840s, suffering a wound in the thigh. In October 1861, soon after the start of the Civil War, he was promoted to the rank of major general and thereafter led many units against Union armies. His most famous and controversial role was at Gettysburg in July 1863, where he disagreed with Robert E. Lee's strategy but did his duty and followed the older man's orders. He stayed with Lee throughout the rest of the war, eventually surrendering alongside him.

After the Civil War, Longstreet started a business in New Orleans and switched his political allegiance, endorsing former Union commander Ulysses S. Grant when he ran for president in 1868. In the 1870s, in his brief role as the adjutant general of Louisiana's state militia, he sent a group of black militia soldiers to subdue a riot by white citizens. Already defending himself from criticisms that he had caused the Confederacy to lose the war by not obeying Lee quickly enough, these two moves further damaged Longstreet's reputation with his fellow Southerners. Concerned for the safety of himself and his family, Longstreet moved from New Orleans to Georgia in 1875. He held several government positions throughout his life, including a one-year stint as the US ambassador to Turkey. He died in 1904 at the age of 82.

His dread was well founded. In the war's most famous single assault—known to history as "Pickett's Charge"—the attackers threw themselves against the wall of Union men and guns.

More than half the men who took part in Pickett's Charge were killed, wounded, or captured—a massacre that crowned the Union victory. Overall, the damages the 164,000 soldiers who fought at Gettysburg inflicted on one another were enormous. On the Confederate side, about 28,000—more than a third of Lee's entire army—were killed, wounded, or missing; Union casualties totaled only slightly less at about 23,000. A few months later, Lincoln traveled to Gettysburg to pay tribute to the soldiers and the cause for which many of them had died—national unity. His famous speech later became known as the Gettysburg Address.

FROM THE SOURCE: A CONFEDERATE SOLDIER'S ACCOUNT

A Confederate soldier wrote this graphic account of the extreme pain and suffering of the wounded men who were lying in wagons in the aftermath of the battle at Gettysburg:

> *Their torn and bloody clothing, matted and hardened, was rasping the tender, inflamed, and still oozing wounds ... From near every wagon ... came cries such as these: "Oh my God, why can't I die?" "My God, will no one have mercy and kill me?" "Stop! Oh! For God's sake, stop just one minute, take me out and leave me to die by the roadside" ... During this one night I realized more of the horrors of war than I had in the preceding two years.*[1]

1. Quoted in Rachel F. Seidman, ed., *The Civil War: A History in Documents* (New York, NY: Oxford University Press, 2001), p. 111.

The Bravery of Black Soldiers

About two weeks after the fateful struggle at Gettysburg, still another important turning point occurred when a unit of black soldiers made history. In the war's early years, Union officials had not allowed black soldiers to fight. Beginning in August 1862, some black men did serve as guards in small towns in border states, but they did not see action.

The first black combat units in the Union army were established in late 1862 and early 1863. In Union-occupied Louisiana, Benjamin F. Butler, the administrator of New Orleans, raised a small unit of black soldiers who fought in the siege of Port Hudson on May 27, 1863. A Union officer who witnessed the assault testified,

Black soldiers played an important role in the eventual Union victory. Shown here is the Fourth Colored Infantry at Fort Lincoln in 1865.

"These men did not swerve or show cowardice. I have been in several [battles] and I never before beheld such coolness and daring."[6]

Meanwhile, Colonel Higginson's First South Carolina Volunteers had been organizing and drilling. In his now-classic *Army Life in a Black Regiment*, written after the war, Higginson praised the discipline and professionalism of his black recruits, saying, "Since I have taken command, I have heard of no man intoxicated, and there has been but one small quarrel. I suppose that scarcely a white regiment in the army shows so little swearing ... Nor are [the black troops] lazy, either about work or drill."[7]

The American public was largely unaware of the qualities shown by black soldiers until the attack on South Carolina's Fort Wagner on July 18, 1863. The black soldiers who took part were members of the 54th Massachusetts Volunteer Infantry Regiment. It had been organized early in 1863 by that state's governor, John A. Andrew, who also handpicked its commander, Colonel Robert Gould Shaw. The troops were recruited—mostly from Massachusetts and other Northern states—by abolitionists. Most of the black men who fought at Fort Wagner had never been slaves; they had been born free in the North. Many of them were fighting largely for the black people in the South who had been freed on paper but still suffered in slavery with no one to enforce the Emancipation Proclamation.

The 54th saw its first action on July 16, when it lost 42 men driving back a Confederate charge on James Island, South Carolina. The remaining 600 men in the unit, with Shaw himself in the lead, stormed nearby Fort Wagner, a Confederate facility in Charleston, two days later. The fantastic show of fighting skills and sheer courage displayed by these troops shattered several myths of black inferiority and worthlessness. After that, both whites and blacks knew that black soldiers could and would fight to end the institution of slavery.

After the extraordinarily bloody fight, 102 of the men from the 54th, including Shaw, were dead or missing; another 179 were wounded or captured. They did not manage to take the fort, but their heroic effort gained them eternal fame and honor. It also encouraged more black enlistment in the army, which Lincoln later said was an important factor in the overall Union victory. The inscription on a monument raised to them in Boston, Massachusetts, says that their sacrifice gave "undying proof that Americans of African descent possess the pride, courage, and devotion of the patriot soldier."[8] This was part of a huge transformation in American history—the emergence of a class of black citizens who could and would fight for freedom.

How You See History

1. Do you think the Emancipation Proclamation had any real effect on the slaves? Explain your answer.
2. Why was the Battle of Gettysburg so important?
3. If you were in Lincoln's place, do you think saving the Union would have been as important to you? If not, what would your main goal have been?

CHAPTER FOUR

IN THE FIELD AND AT HOME

The Civil War was not the first war in United States history, but it was the first to take place after the Industrial Revolution. This meant that the weapons that were available were far different—and deadlier—than anyone had used in the past. This was a big part of why the Civil War caused such a high number of casualties.

Rifles, with their long-range capabilities, had already replaced muskets. This meant soldiers did not have to be close to the enemy to fire, and the opposition could be killed from farther away. New kinds of ammunition—especially cone-shaped bullets called Minié balls—allowed rifles to be loaded in less time and without the aid of devices such as ramrods. It is estimated that rifles with Minié bullets were responsible for about 90 percent of all Civil War casualties.

The repeating rifle, which could fire more than one bullet before needing to be reloaded, emerged during the war. This technology was produced by the North, which gave the Union another advantage. New kinds of cannons also added to battlefield destruction.

New Guns

One of the most important technological advances in weaponry during the Civil War was a slow but steady transition from old-style, often inaccurate handheld firearms to more reliable and accurate ones. When the conflict began in 1861, a large proportion of the

◀ Shown here are authentic Minié ball fragments.

guns in use were already outdated. Soldiers using them were less able to defend themselves and were more likely to be killed by the enemy. Many of the old-fashioned weapons were replaced by more advanced models during the war, but not before the outdated guns caused many unnecessary deaths.

The oldest handheld guns used in the war were called "smoothbore" muskets because they had a long barrel whose bore, or hollow inside, had a smooth surface. One common model, which had first been made in 1816, featured a barrel about 57 inches (145 centimeters) long and a caliber (the width of the bore) of 0.69 inch (1.8 cm). Another musket widely used in the Civil War dated from 1840 but was no more advanced or reliable. These were called muzzleloaders; a soldier loaded one by inserting a musket ball (a rounded piece of lead) into the muzzle, or front, of the barrel.

Shown here is a Civil War reenactor holding a Springfield rifle, which was the most common type of gun used during the war.

Smoothbore and muzzleloader muskets were outdated because they had an old-fashioned firing mechanism called a flintlock, which required several steps to load. When the operator pulled the trigger, a piece of flint hit a steel plate, producing a spark that ignited some gunpowder in a small pan mounted in the back of the weapon. A soldier could load and fire effectively only about twice per minute, although sometimes the gun failed to fire at all. In addition, the flintlock musket was noticeably inaccurate beyond a range of a couple hundred feet (approximately 60 m).

Another handheld firearm used extensively in the Civil War, called the rifle musket, was more accurate and had greater range. The term "rifle" comes from "rifling," a set of spiral grooves cut into the inside walls of the barrel. When someone fired a rifle, the ball spiraled through the grooves and exited the gun spinning, producing a more accurate shot. The US Army ordered production of a muzzle-loading, .58-caliber rifle musket in 1855. At the start of the Civil War, however, this weapon made up only about 10 percent of all the handheld guns in American arsenals. To fix this shortage, the US armory in Springfield, Massachusetts, began making a new model in 1861. Nicknamed the "Springfield" because of where it was produced, this gun became the most common handheld firearm used in the war. At the same time, the South began manufacturing a similar weapon at its armories in Fayetteville, North Carolina, and Richmond, Virginia.

An even more reliable and faster-loading firearm was available in 1861. Called the Sharps rifle after its inventor, American mechanic Christian Sharps, it loaded through the breech, or rear, instead of the muzzle. A foot soldier carrying this weapon could fire six to nine shots per minute. However, because the Union officer in charge of acquiring firearms, James W. Ripley, was old-fashioned and did not trust newer weapons, very few Sharps rifles were used by infantry (foot soldiers) in the war. Fortunately for the North, Ripley did eventually order 80,000 Sharps .52-caliber rifles for the Union cavalry (troops on horseback).

HISTORY HAPPENED HERE: SPRINGFIELD, MASSACHUSETTS

Today, Springfield is popular with tourists for many reasons. One is the Basketball Hall of Fame, which is located in Springfield because that's where James Naismith invented the game in 1891—less than 30 years after the end of the Civil War. Another is the Dr. Seuss Museum. One of Seuss's books, *And to Think That I Saw It on Mulberry Street*, was inspired by a street of the same name that still exists in Springfield.

History buffs may enjoy visiting the Springfield Armory National Historic Site, where arms were produced for the US government from 1777 to 1968. The armory is now a museum that showcases various kinds of weapons that were made there and used in American wars, including the Springfield rifle that was commonly used in the Civil War. The museum frequently holds concerts and other special events to give visitors a unique historical experience.

Heavy Weapons

In addition to handheld firearms, Civil War soldiers and units used larger, heavier, more destructive guns. The general name for them is cannons, but they are more precisely called heavy ordnance or artillery. A group of soldiers who operated one or more such weapons was called an artillery battery. The Union's superior industrial capacity allowed it to maintain a major edge over the Confederacy in artillery production throughout the war. A Confederate officer named Edward P. Alexander later recalled that Southern arsenals lacked enough supplies of metals to make artillery as well as "the mechanical skill necessary to turn out first-class ammunition."[1]

Artillery ammunition did different and more extensive sorts of damage. For example, a shell—a hollowed-out cannonball containing gunpowder—sent pieces of its surface flying in all directions. Shells also caused secondary explosions when they ignited ammunition stores. In contrast, spherical case (also called shrapnel or grapeshot) and canister shot were metal containers that held many small lead or iron musket balls. These scattered in all directions after a fuse ignited a charge of gunpowder packed inside.

Union and Confederate artillery gunners alike used two principal types of artillery—"guns" and howitzers. Both were cast from iron or bronze and could be either smoothbore or rifled. One major

Shown here are two Civil War soldiers posing with howitzer cannons.

difference between the two types was that the gun had a long barrel in relation to its caliber and was most often used to target objects in plain sight.

The second main kind of field artillery, the howitzer, fired only shells, case, and canister. Also, a howitzer could fire at a higher angle than a gun, which made it more effective for sending projectiles over trees, houses, low hills, and other obstacles. However, it did have a disadvantage: The operators' inability to see the target clearly made the howitzer less accurate than the gun.

Shortly before the Civil War began, the Union army created an artillery weapon that combined some of the advantages of both a gun and a howitzer. It was called the Napoleon, after the famous French general who used artillery successfully in Europe in the early 1800s. The Napoleon was a smoothbore artillery gun that could fire shells at a higher angle than a normal gun. It became the most widely used cannon of the Civil War. The Union made 1,131 of them, compared to 630 produced by the Confederacy.

Rifled cannons and mortars were also used in the conflict. Both sides used Parrott guns—named after their inventor, Robert Parrott—which had rifled barrels. Parrott guns were more accurate than Napoleons, but their barrels sometimes exploded, causing injuries and deaths among the gunners. The mortar was mainly a siege cannon. It was short, stumpy, and fired at a very high angle, allowing its shells to fly over the high walls of forts and fortified towns. The most widely used mortar of the Civil War was the Coehorn. It had a barrel about 16 inches (40.6 cm) long and fired shells weighing 17 pounds (7.7 kilograms) as far as 1,200 yards (1,097 m). The sounds made by firing mortars were loud and frightening enough to make the enemy flee, abandoning their own guns.

Organizing the Armies

Handheld guns, artillery, and other weapons in the Civil War were used mainly by foot soldiers who fought on land, most often to capture and hold enemy territory. Their success depended on more than the quality of their arms, however. The effectiveness of their organization and tactics was also crucial.

Regarding organization, both the Union and Confederate armies broke down into standard units. The basic infantry unit was the regiment, which under ideal conditions, numbered about 1,000 men. However, conditions were often far from ideal; sickness, death, desertion, and other factors frequently caused infantry regiments to be shorthanded. In reality, most regiments had 500 or fewer men. The average regiment had 10 companies—ideally with 100 men each, but more often with 40 to 50 men. A brigade was made up of 3 to 6 regiments; a division was made up of 2 or 3 brigades; about 3 divisions made up a corps; and several corps made up an army (for example, the Union's Army of the Potomac). Maintaining a unit's cohesion, or structure and unity, in combat situations was crucial. When such cohesion broke down, Ian Drury wrote, the unit "was doomed to defeat at the hands of a better organized enemy," and the result could be "a long casualty list with little to show for it."[2]

Although the tactics used by regiments and other units varied widely, two general categories of tactics were seen most often. The first tactic involved attacking in successive waves, and it was used when armies faced each other in the open. Typically, each wave was made up of a double line of men separated, ideally, from the waves in front and behind it by about 200 yards (183 m). Under real combat conditions, however, the waves often slowed down and bunched up, creating a larger, less organized mass of men. Each attacking wave fired a volley at the enemy. If the enemy did not retreat, the attackers fired more volleys. The enemy fired back, of course, and this relatively close-range exchange was called a firefight. When the opposing troops' ammunition was gone or they were too tired to continue, it was common for each side to fall back.

The other major kind of battlefield tactic employed in the conflict is most commonly called trench warfare. It consisted of building, defending, and attacking fieldworks, which were mainly fortified trenches. A typical version was 4 to 6 feet (1.2 to 1.8 m) deep with the excavated soil piled up in front as a protective barrier. The most elaborate examples had logs, wooden planks, tunnels, and hollowed-out chambers. The primary motive for such fieldworks

Shown here are Union soldiers in trenches near Petersburg, Virginia.

was not defensive, however, but rather to force the enemy to attack in the open, in front of the trenches, where soldiers were most vulnerable. The result of such assaults, which were common in the war, was heavy casualties.

Cavalry played a considerably smaller role in the Civil War than the infantry did. This was partly because neither the Union nor Confederacy supplied the money and other resources necessary for creating huge, powerful cavalry units like those that had fought in the Napoleonic Wars in Europe a few decades before. Nevertheless, both the North and South did employ units of horsemen with great effectiveness in certain situations.

The most important of these was gathering and delivering vital military information. Despite the use of the telegraph and spies, commanders came to rely on fast, mobile horsemen to scout enemy forces and report back. Another highly effective use of cavalry in the war was raiding enemy territory to disrupt communication and supply lines and create fear among the civilians.

FROM THE SOURCE: IN THE TRENCHES

When Union troops charged Confederate trenches at Cold Harbor, near Richmond, in early June 1864, a massacre ensued. According to a Confederate officer who took part:

> *The charging column ... [was hit by] the most destructive fire I ever saw ... In two minutes not a man of them was standing ... The stench from the dead between our lines and theirs was sickening ... The dead covered more than five acres of ground about as thickly as they could be laid.*[1]

1. William C. Oates, *The War Between the Union and the Confederacy and Its Lost Opportunities* (New York, NY: Neale Publishing, 1905), p. 367.

So many people died during the war that it was sometimes difficult to identify the bodies. Shown here is the grave of an unknown Confederate soldier.

In addition, Civil War cavalry units could launch charges against enemy positions, though this rarely happened. Such assaults were also typically on a small scale, with a few dozen or at most a few hundred horsemen taking part, and they were largely ineffective.

Spying on the Enemy

Both the North and South found espionage, or spying, to be very effective in the war and used this tactic frequently. When the conflict began, neither side had a clear idea about how to organize an intelligence-gathering operation. However, they both recognized the potential of espionage and quickly developed successful networks of spies.

THEY MADE HISTORY: ELIZABETH VAN LEW

Elizabeth "Bet" Van Lew was a successful Union spy who ran her espionage operation in the Confederate capital, Richmond. Having been educated in Philadelphia, Pennsylvania, she grew up with strong abolitionist views. She regularly brought baskets of food, medicine, and books to Union prisoners held in Libby Prison in Richmond and managed to gather information about Confederate troop movements from newly arrived Northern soldiers. She led other spies as well, who went places she was unable to go and passed information back to her. One of these was Mary Jane Richards Denman, a black woman who worked in Jefferson Davis's home to gather information for the Union. General Grant later remarked that Van Lew's intelligence was the most valuable he received during the war. After the war, she was given the position of postmistress of Richmond from 1869 to 1877, after which she worked as a clerk in Washington, DC's, Post Office Department. However, even after her service to her country, Van Lew—like other women of the time period—was never given the right to vote.

Many of these spies were women. Probably the most renowned was Rose O'Neal Greenhow, who eventually gained the nickname "Rebel Rose." Because her husband worked for the US State Department before the war, she had many government connections, which she used to aid the Confederacy after the war began. Though earnest and daring, Greenhow was often careless, and Union agents arrested her early in the conflict.

Both sides also benefited from the services of male spies. Lincoln himself recruited William A. Lloyd, a New York publisher of steamboat guides and maps of Southern states, to spy for the Union. Lloyd and an associate, Thomas Boyd, collected much valuable information about the Confederacy.

Meanwhile, a Confederate spy, Thomas H. Hines—nicknamed "the Fox"—gathered intelligence about the North. Hines also hatched a daring plan to sabotage Northern cities, murder several Northern leaders, and set fire to Chicago, Illinois, as well as New York City. The scheme failed due to a lack of resources and mistakes made by some of his helpers. Nevertheless, Hines did manage to create a fair amount of fear and disruption in the North. He was also part of a threatening bigger picture. The extensive use of spies in the conflict foreshadowed the even larger international spy networks of the 20th century. This is another reason why the Civil War is sometimes called the first modern war.

On the Home Front

The Civil War changed more than just the way battles were fought; it also changed the way people lived. Those left behind on the home front contributed what they could to their side. Women made flags and clothing for soldiers. Farmers gathered crops to feed the troops. However, people also had to continue working at businesses and on farms. Women and children sometimes had to take on jobs that had been filled by men who were now soldiers. Still, families often struggled to bring in enough money to feed themselves. Food was especially scarce near places where the Union and Confederate forces were stationed because the armies took the resources to meet their own needs. Families too close to the fighting sometimes relocated, but the poor could not leave their homes and livelihoods behind.

The major dedication of time and energy to the war effort is well illustrated by the changing nature of work and employment. As in ages past, a majority of families in America in the early 1800s made their living by farming. However, just prior to the Civil War, this situation was already undergoing a rapid transformation. The main agent of change was the growth of urban centers and industry, particularly in the North. Then, the war's beginning created many new industrial jobs, including mass production of weapons, uniforms, shoes, wagons, ships, and so forth. In Philadelphia alone, 58 factories opened in 1862 and another 57 the following year.

Hoping to be hired for some of the newly created jobs, large numbers of Northerners left their farms and migrated to the cities. At the same time, about 250,000 foreign immigrants, mostly from Europe, arrived in the North each year during the war. (Roughly a fifth of the Union's 19 to 20 million inhabitants were foreign born at the time.) They, too, competed in the expanding job market.

To accommodate so many new workers, Northern cities had to expand at dizzying rates. Construction of new streets, houses, churches, shops, and schools struggled to keep pace. The majority of workers made barely enough money to stay alive, so they were forced to live in the hundreds of vast, crowded, gloomy tenements that sprang up around the factories. It was common for eight to ten people to live in a single-room apartment that lacked both central heating and plumbing facilities. "Outside the tenement was a trench a foot or two deep for a toilet,"[3] historian Donald D. Jackson wrote. Moreover, the alleys between the tenements were poorly lit and filthy. In 1863, at the height of the war, almost half of New York City's population—about 400,000 people—lived in such conditions.

Despite the migration of Northern farmworkers to the cities, Northern agriculture actually thrived during the war. One reason for this was that the wives and children of men who had gone off to fight worked double-time to take up the slack. Also, industry was supplying new commercial fertilizers and laborsaving

This woodcut shows how crowded and uncomfortable many New York City dwellings had become—especially for people with little money—by the late 1860s.

mowing and reaping machines that vastly increased efficiency and crop production.

On the Confederate home front, meanwhile, where industrialization was insignificant, most Southerners remained farmers. However, very few of them fit the stereotype of the well-to-do plantation owner with vast fields worked by hundreds of slaves. In fact, wealthy Southern plantation owners made up only one-half of 1 percent of the Confederacy's 9 million people. A far larger proportion—about 50 percent—worked farms of 100 or fewer acres. In addition, about 2 million, or almost a quarter, of Southerners were part-time farmers who also made a living hunting and fishing.

No matter how rich or poor Southern farmers were, all believed in one guiding principle: Working one's land—in contrast to working on a machine, the way people in the North did—bred in a person a large measure of independence, dignity, and moral values.

Such beliefs quickly created a dilemma for many Southerners. The realities of the war and the effort to win it required them to undergo social changes that seemed to threaten their way of life. For example, industry and commercialism, which most Southerners viewed as unsophisticated, became essential to the creation of a dependable war effort. New Orleans newsman James D. B. DeBow led the push to industrialize the South. He argued that the Confederacy could defeat the Union only if Southerners rapidly built many factories and acquired industrial skills. Some Southern politicians and businessmen heeded DeBow's call and invested money in building factories. A Charleston newspaper optimistically reported, "We shall soon be able to produce every cannon and gun, every pistol and saber, every rifle and spear."[4]

Such enthusiasm proved overblown in the long run, however. The South suffered from a severe labor shortage throughout the war, partly because its population was smaller than that of the North. In addition, as major Southern cities such as New Orleans, Nashville, and Vicksburg steadily fell to Northern armies during the conflict, the Union captured many of the South's newly built factories. As a result, most jobs in the South remained in the agricultural sector.

Problems With Soldiers

Next to making a living, one of the chief concerns of men on the home front was the issue of conscription, or raising troops. To wage a war of such size required the services of millions of soldiers, sailors, and other military personnel. These men had to be recruited, uniformed, and trained. Some men volunteered, while others were drafted; however, some tried to keep from serving, either because they did not want to fight or they objected to the draft. Thus, conscription preoccupied the time and thoughts of large numbers of civilians in both the North and South.

One reason that conscription was a consistently pressing issue was that the authorities were always asking the public to supply more military recruits. In the North, Congress ordered the states to begin drafting men in August 1862. Everyone between the ages of 18 and 45 was eligible except for those who were physically

PAST MEETS PRESENT:
THE RED BADGE OF COURAGE

In 1894, Stephen Crane completed his Civil War novel, *The Red Badge of Courage*. This book tells the story of 18-year-old soldier Henry Fleming's war experiences. Through Fleming's eyes, Crane muses on the concepts of courage and cowardice; for example, during his first encounter with Confederate soldiers, Fleming runs away in fear, although he later returns to his regiment. In later battles, Fleming acts more courageously and feels as though this makes up for his previous cowardice.

Since its initial publication, *The Red Badge of Courage* has been very popular, although some people—especially war veterans—criticized Crane for writing it when he had never been a soldier. Several film adaptations have also been made; the best-known one was released in 1951 and is popular with Civil War buffs.

Shown here is the movie poster for the 1951 version of *The Red Badge of Courage*.

disabled or worked in crucial jobs, such as telegraph operators or munitions workers. Some states offered cash rewards called bounties to persuade men to join up. This sometimes resulted in "bounty jumpers": individuals who collected the money but then fled to another state. A number of other men who did not want to serve damaged themselves by cutting off some of their fingers or yanking out their teeth. To shame these draft dodgers, many Northern towns published their names on "coward lists" in newspapers.

Despite such draft resistance, Northern states did manage to enlist large numbers of men. However, as battlefield casualties continued to climb, Lincoln saw the necessity of instituting a federal draft in 1863. There was even more resistance to it than there had been to the state-run version. It ended in a series of bloody riots, the most famous of which occurred in New York City. On July 13, 1863, angry crowds burned down local draft offices, attacked policemen, and invaded private homes. In all, at least 100 people were killed. Still, the resisters proved to be in the minority. Overall, Northerners responded with patriotism, viewing the draft as a necessary evil.

On the Southern home front, many people supported the Confederate cause and willingly joined the army. However, like in the North, others were reluctant, and some went to great lengths to avoid serving. One reason was a lack of sympathy for the Confederacy's principal ideals, especially slavery, which some Southerners felt was wrong. Furthermore, even though most Southerners viewed black people as inferior to whites, many did not own slaves and were not ready to fight and die so that a few well-off Southerners could keep their slaves.

Such attitudes across the Confederate home front caused enlistments to drop off steadily early in the war. In response, the Confederate Congress enacted a mandatory military draft in April 1862. This law was widely unpopular, and many Southern men tried to evade it. Some did so legally, since the law in both the North and the South at that time allowed a man to pay someone else to serve for him. Others used illegal methods, such as falsely claiming they were too ill to serve, paying someone to make fake discharge papers, or simply failing to show up for duty. Historians estimate that almost half of Southern men who were drafted never showed up. This was surely one of the major reasons that the Confederacy's chances of winning the war decreased over time—a grim reality not lost on Southern generals.

Not Just a Man's War

While many men on the home front were wrestling with the issue of conscription, many women in both the North and the South faced new challenges, including making sacrifices for the war effort and taking jobs that supported it. Lincoln recognized the enormous contributions women made, saying, "If all that has been said by orators and poets since the creation of the world were applied to the women of America, it would not do them justice for their conduct during this war."[5]

One of the most direct roles played by women in the conflict was as "matrons of the regiment." These soldiers' wives staffed army camps—both near and far from battlefields—acting as cooks, secretaries, laundresses, and nurses. In mid-1861, a group of concerned New York women established the US Sanitary Commission, which was an early version of the American Red Cross. The commission organized the making of bandages and clothing for the troops, the collection of medical supplies and food, and the cleaning of army camps and hospitals. Working from dawn to dusk in a makeshift hospital on the Gettysburg battlefield, nurse Cornelia Hancock wrote in July 1863, "If it was not for the Sanitary [Commission], much suffering would ensue … We have plenty of woolen blankets now [supplied by the Commission], but for about five days after the battle, the men had no blankets nor scarce any shelter."[6] Other notable contributions to nursing during the war were made by Dorothea Dix of Maine and Clara Barton of Massachusetts. Dix became the superintendent of nurses for the Union army, and Barton founded an agency that distributed supplies to the troops. Later, she was also in charge of organizing searches for soldiers missing in action.

Many other Northern women worked in factories, as store clerks, and in offices. Thousands labored up to 15 hours a day sewing uniforms for soldiers and clothes for civilians. They were extremely

Many women made important contributions during the Civil War, but few were given credit. Dorothea Dix is one of the women whose names became well known.

underpaid and at times had trouble collecting their wages. As a result, seamstresses in Boston, Chicago, and other major cities started organizing unions to represent their interests.

Meanwhile, across the South, many women managed farms and plantations while their husbands were away fighting. Smaller numbers of women were involved in small-scale manufacturing, especially the kind that helped the war effort. Southerner Catherine Edmondston noted in her diary, "Ladies who never worked before are hard at work making uniforms and tents."[7] Southern women also worked as government clerks, nurses, and teachers.

Being Black During the Civil War

Many white men and women in both the North and the South made low wages and lived in poor conditions. Even so, they were generally better off than most black people on the home front. This was because the vast majority of black people in the South were slaves, and most free black people living in the North were routinely targeted by racism.

The troubles of slaves in the South before and during the Civil War have been heavily documented in written accounts and dramatized in films. Most slaves lived in shacks with few or no basic amenities and were subject to harsh discipline, including brutal whippings. In addition, some slave families were permanently broken up when masters sold off fathers, mothers, or children to other owners, and large numbers of female slaves were sexually abused by their masters.

The abuses suffered by free black people in the North in the Civil War era are less well known, but some accounts do exist. Many Northerners may have opposed slavery, but this was largely an economic issue to them, not a humanitarian one. Northern whites viewed black people as lazy, dishonest, and immoral, and they frequently discriminated against them. For example, only three Northern states—Massachusetts, Maine, and New Hampshire—gave black men full voting rights. Most Northern black people were also segregated into inferior shantytowns and slums. A white man who visited a black slum in Washington, DC, in 1864 described people living in tarpaper huts separated by filthy, rat-infested alleyways. "The weather is cold," he said, and the residents "have little or no wood" for fires. He continued, "Snow covers the ground and they have a scanty supply of rags called clothes. [The] government gives them a very, very small allowance of soup."[8]

Some Northern missionaries and charitable organizations did try to help improve the conditions black people were living in, especially in Union-occupied parts of the South. In particular, they printed books and other materials designed to teach freed slaves and other illiterate black people how to read and write. They also set up and ran schools for black children. This aspect of life on the Civil War home front foreshadowed momentous changes in the future.

How You See History

1. How might the war have gone differently if soldiers had access to modern-day weapons?
2. Why do you think so many people tried to avoid fighting in the war?
3. Why do you think Northerners opposed slavery yet treated black people so poorly?

CHAPTER FIVE

THE END OF THE CONFEDERACY

Although 1863 marked a turning point in the war, the conflict was far from over. The Union was determined not to give up and planned to do whatever was necessary to put an end to the Confederate States of America, but the South continued to fight back. Ulysses S. Grant's successes had won him a promotion to general-in-chief of the Union armies, and he was coming up with a new plan.

Grant's strategy was essentially to crush the Southern armies. Union forces would attack different key areas at the same time, destroying not just the military but also the resources that were still keeping the Confederacy afloat: their farms, their railroads, and even their cities. This tactic was infamously demonstrated by Major General William T. Sherman's March to the Sea. Confederate forces were already stretched to the limit, but Grant saw to it that there was no break in the action for them. There was still much bloodshed to come.

Another Siege

Grant realized that capturing the Confederate capital of Richmond, Virginia, and its surrounding territories would deal the South a debilitating blow from which it likely could not recover. In Grant's

◀ Ulysses S. Grant (*shown here*) and the new strategy he came up with were instrumental in securing a Northern victory.

mind, the most effective way to take Richmond was first to capture its chief local supply base. This was the town of Petersburg, located about 23 miles (37 km) south of the capital. Petersburg also rested at the junction of five Confederate railroad lines that carried supplies to and from the Carolinas and other Southern states.

The Siege of Petersburg began on June 15, 1864. It was not a siege in the traditional sense, but rather an enormous and long-lasting example of trench warfare. Union soldiers dug about 30 miles (48 km) of trenches around Petersburg's southern rim, and Robert E. Lee's men built opposing trenches, creating a standoff. Over the months that followed, at least 19 small but bloody battles were fought in the area as each side competed for control of the region.

One of the most memorable of these engagements was the Battle of the Crater, which took place on July 30, 1864. A group of former Pennsylvania coal miners dug a Union tunnel 511 feet (156 m) long under some of the Confederate trenches. They then placed explosives in the tunnel and detonated them, creating a crater that averaged 135 feet (41 m) in width.

About 280 Confederate soldiers were immediately killed in the blast. When Union troops followed up, they moved into the crater rather than around its rim. This was a fatal mistake because they became trapped and subject to a deadly rain of enemy gunfire from above. "There was the whole Ninth Corps crowded into a space where there was barely enough room for one division to operate," one of the Union officers later reported. "And there we stood … hour after hour, under a plunging fire from the Confederate guns."[1] A total of 4,400 Union soldiers were killed, wounded, or captured in the fight. Despite this Northern defeat, however, Grant's forces maintained their chokehold on Petersburg and continued to drain Richmond of essential supplies.

Extreme Measures

While the Union campaign in eastern Virginia was happening, the North's other strategic assaults on the Confederacy went forward. One principal target was the Shenandoah Valley in western Virginia—one of the South's most productive agricultural

HISTORY HAPPENED HERE: PETERSBURG, VIRGINIA

As the site of the longest Civil War battle, Petersburg is a popular place for tourists who are interested in the war's history. Petersburg National Battlefield is free to visit, and an app is available to help visitors take a self-guided tour. Park rangers at the visitor center are also generally available to answer questions. The crater the Union soldiers created by blowing up Confederate trenches is still visible, although it is not as dramatic as some might expect; over the years, weather has eroded its edges and vegetation has grown back, making it look more like a natural dip in the land.

Visitors to Petersburg can also tour a plantation and visit Henricus Historical Park for a peek further back into the region's history. This site recreates an English military fort and a Native American village as they would have appeared when Virginia was a British colony. Additionally, the Prince George County Regional Heritage Center looks at how the area has changed from prehistoric times to today, paying special attention to the various cultures of the people who have settled there.

Shown here are tourists visiting the Petersburg crater two years after the end of the Civil War.

regions. Major General Philip Sheridan led the Union's forces in what became known as the Valley Campaigns between May and October 1864. After defeating Confederate general Jubal A. Early in a series of battles, including the decisive Battle of Cedar Creek on October 19, 1864, Sheridan laid waste to most of the valley's prime farmlands.

Farther south, Sherman marched his army from Tennessee into Georgia. His main objective was to take the important Southern city of Atlanta in Georgia. Confederate general Joseph E. Johnston harassed the Union advance and even scored a narrow victory in the Battle of Kennesaw Mountain on June 27, 1864. However, Johnston was unable to stop Sherman, who plunged ahead toward Atlanta. A troubled Jefferson Davis replaced Johnston with Lieutenant General John B. Hood, who was only 33 years old at the time—the youngest man to command an army for either side in the conflict. Hood, however, also failed to halt the Union onslaught, and Sherman captured Atlanta on September 2.

This picture shows part of Atlanta, Georgia, after Sherman's troops set it on fire.

FROM THE SOURCE: SHERMAN'S RESPONSE

When the mayor of Atlanta begged Sherman not to burn the city, Sherman gave the following answer, which summarized the grim realities all Southerners now faced:

> *We must stop the war that now desolates our once happy and favored country. To stop the war, we must defeat the rebel armies which are arrayed against the law and Constitution that all must respect and obey ... You cannot qualify war in harsher terms than I will. War is cruelty, and you cannot refine it ... You might as well appeal against the thunderstorm as against these terrible hardships of war. They are inevitable ... We don't want your Negroes, or your horses, or your houses, or your lands [but] we do want and will have a just obedience to the laws of the United States ... and if it involves the destruction of your [property], we cannot help it.*[1]

1. Quoted in Rachel F. Seidman, ed., *The Civil War: A History in Documents* (New York, NY: Oxford University Press, 2001), p. 112.

Sherman next planned to march his troops eastward to the coastal city of Savannah, about 300 miles (483 km) away. To ensure that Atlanta would not fall back into enemy hands, he ordered his men to evacuate and torch the city. One Union soldier later described the burning of Atlanta as "a grand and awful spectacle" in which "the heaven is one expanse of lurid fire; the air is filled with flying, burning cinders; buildings covering two hundred acres are in ruins or in flames."[2]

Sherman's "March to the Sea" has become legendary. On their way to Savannah, his troops destroyed at least 20 percent of Georgia's farms. The Confederate army tried to fight back, but it was no use. Sherman marched on, with almost no obstacles in his way, to Savannah, which surrendered on December 21, 1864.

Cutting Off the South

Lincoln approved Grant and Sherman's next decision, which was a continuation of their strategy of crushing the Confederacy's means and will to carry on the fight. The Union blockade of Southern ports grew tighter, drying up vital Confederate supply lines. At the same time, the North destroyed or seized Southern railroad lines to deny the South other important supplies. Food shortages became so serious that some Southerners killed and ate their plow animals to avoid starvation, while others resorted to stealing to make ends meet. Most could not have afforded to buy much even if store shelves had been full because the value of Confederate currency had dropped to one-fortieth its face value, making it nearly worthless.

Meanwhile, the South's manpower shortages went from bad to worse. By the end of 1864, most of the men who were drafted tried to avoid military service, and in that same period, about 70,000 Confederate soldiers deserted their units. Desperate, the government began drafting boys ages 14 to 18 and men ages 45 to 60. Though these recruits were mostly assigned to guard duty to free up other soldiers for actual combat, the move was widely unpopular. One critic described it as "robbing the cradle and the grave to supply Lee's army."[3]

In the face of quickly shrinking Confederate manpower, even the usually calm Lee could see that only a miracle could save the South from utter defeat. Early in 1865, Lee went so far as to call for restoring the army's ranks by arming Southern black men to fight for the Confederacy. These soldiers, he suggested, would be given their freedom as a reward for their service. Many Southerners intensely rejected this idea, but the Confederate Congress saw no other choice; on March 13, 1865, it passed a bill ordering the mobilization of about 300,000 black slaves.

However, none of these men ever ended up fighting for the South. The siege at Petersburg had continued over the winter and early spring, steadily wearing down the strength and morale of Lee's troops. He was finally forced to abandon both Petersburg and Richmond. The Confederate capital fell on April 3, 1865. Before leaving the city, Southern troops torched cotton and food supplies so the incoming army would not be able to use them. As the fires spread, they gutted large sections of the city.

Surrender at Appomattox

After retreating from Petersburg and Richmond, Lee led the remnants of his army toward North Carolina, where he hoped to join up with Joseph Johnston's remaining forces and make a last stand against the enemy. Instead, Philip Sheridan intercepted some of Lee's contingents at Sayler's Creek, southwest of Petersburg, on April 6. The Confederates were disastrously defeated. Large numbers of them surrendered, including Lee's son, Major General Curtis Lee.

Robert E. Lee now assessed the situation and concluded that further resistance and bloodshed were pointless. When he received a message from General Grant the next day asking that he surrender, he agreed and asked what Grant's terms of surrender were. Grant said that all Confederate officers and men could return to their homes and would be free from prosecution for treason as long as they promised not to take up arms against the US government again—a generous offer.

The historic surrender took place on April 9, 1865, in the McLean House in the small Virginia hamlet of Appomattox Court House. Lee arrived at 1 p.m., about half an hour before Grant. Although his side had won, Grant later wrote that he felt "sad" at seeing "the downfall of a foe who had fought so long and valiantly and had suffered so much."[4] Lee asked if his men could keep their horses, and Grant agreed to allow it so the animals could be used to raise much-needed crops across the South. Relieved, Lee said, "This will have the best possible effect upon the men" and "will do much toward conciliating our people."[5]

After the meeting ended, Lee met with some of his troops, most of whom were distraught. Instead of blaming Lee, they expressed "their willingness to submit at once, or fight to the last man, as he ordered."[6] However, Lee knew the fight was over; his side had lost, and he was determined to respect that. "I have done for you all that was in my power to do," he told his men. "You have all done your

This picture illustrates the historic surrender of Robert E. Lee (*middle left*) at Appomattox Court House.

duty. Leave the result to God. Go to your homes and resume your occupations. Obey the laws and become as good citizens as you were soldiers."[7]

Back in Washington, DC, the president soon received word of the surrender, which had effectively ended the war. Technically, Lee had surrendered only his own army, but it was widely understood that the Confederacy had been shattered and could not win. Abraham Lincoln, looking older than his years because of the enormous weight of his office, breathed a huge sigh of relief. Four years before, he had set forth a clear, unwavering goal—to save the Union. Through his masterful leadership, supported by the personal sacrifices of hundreds of thousands of American soldiers and civilians, he had achieved this challenging goal. However, he did not live to see the official end of the war. Lincoln was assassinated by actor John Wilkes Booth on April 14, 1865, only five days after Lee surrendered. Jefferson Davis was captured on May 10, 1865, and the final official battle of the Civil War was fought two days later at Palmito Ranch, Texas. Although the Confederates won that

THEY MADE HISTORY: ROBERT E. LEE

Robert E. Lee came from a prominent Virginian family, but despite his family's societal connections, they were not wealthy. Because he could not afford to go to college, Lee went instead to the military academy at West Point, where he distinguished himself and won the respect of his classmates with his kindness and dignity. After he graduated, he served as a captain in the Mexican-American War. In April 1861, the federal government asked him to lead the Union army, but Lee refused because although he did not support secession, he also did not want to be part of an invasion of the South—especially his home state of Virginia. When his state voted to secede, he resigned from the Union army and became the commander of Virginia's forces.

Throughout the war, Lee never had much hope that the Confederate forces could overcome the Union ones. He knew the North had better resources and more soldiers, so he hoped to simply keep them at bay long enough for them to get discouraged and give up. He scored several victories, but eventually his shrinking army as well as food and clothing shortages took their toll. After the war, he accepted the post of president of Washington College in Lexington, Virginia, where he remained until his death in 1870. Despite the fact that he was a military general and fought for the South, he disapproved of war as a way to settle political problems.

battle, they had already lost the war. The official end came on June 2, 1865, when the Army of the Trans-Mississippi agreed to terms of surrender.

After the War

In some ways, the immediate aftermath of the American Civil War was almost as divisive and bloody as the conflict itself. Bitter animosities and divisions marked the postwar period generally referred to as Reconstruction, which had two major aspects. The first was to politically reintegrate the formerly seceded Southern states into the Union. The second was to rebuild the devastated South. The human toll alone had been tremendous—as much as 10 percent of the 2.5 million Southern white males were killed, and hundreds of thousands more were wounded or injured. In addition, Richmond, Atlanta, and dozens of other Southern towns lay in ruins; people had lost their homes, and in general, the Southern economy was in shambles.

The first stage of Reconstruction, which began during the war and lasted until 1866, was controlled by Lincoln at first. After his death, his vice president and successor, Andrew Johnson, took over. Both men favored a moderate approach designed to reunite the opposing sides and quickly heal the nation's wounds; Lincoln had stated in 1864, "Blood cannot restore blood, and the government should not act for revenge."[8] Under their plan, Southern states had to meet certain minimal standards, including repealing secession and ratifying the 13th Amendment to the Constitution, which took the Emancipation Proclamation one step further by abolishing slavery throughout the country. These demands were met by the end of 1865.

In the 1866 elections, however, a group of "radical" Republicans took control of Congress. They thought the presidential-led Reconstruction was too lenient. The same Southern leaders who had led the secession movement had power again and had already enacted "black codes," or laws that severely limited the rights of former slaves. Radical Republicans imposed a much harsher program of restoration, often referred to as Radical Reconstruction. They divided the South into a series of military districts and sent in army units that imposed martial law until new state constitutions were written.

At the same time, "carpetbaggers" descended in large numbers from the North. This is a negative term for businessmen who wanted to economically exploit, or take advantage of, the fractured South. In collaboration with "scalawags"—white Southerners who aided the North and joined the Republican Party—some carpetbaggers benefited from corruption in Southern state governments. Those who

This political cartoon depicts the South as a woman who is being crushed under the weight of a carpetbagger.

opposed Radical Reconstruction used this corruption to overthrow Reconstruction by the mid-1870s. These events generated hostility and bitterness between Southerners and Northerners that survived well into the 20th century and beyond.

Breaking Promises

Another important aspect of Reconstruction that created much bitterness and resentment was its failure to follow through with the promises the government had made to black Americans during the Civil War. On the positive side, black people benefited from the freedom granted by the 13th Amendment. Likewise, the 14th and 15th Amendments, which soon followed, guaranteed them equal protection under the law and voting rights. They also gained the right to be elected to state legislatures and the US Congress.

These reforms were not widely enforced, however. Though slavery was over, most white Southerners still viewed black people as inferiors. The Northern black social reformer Frederick Douglass sadly but correctly foresaw what was coming in a speech to the American Anti-Slavery Society in May 1865:

> *Any wretch may enter the house of a black man and commit any violence he pleases. If he happens to do it only in the presence of black persons, he goes unwhipt of justice … And don't tell me that [Southern whites] have become so just and honest all at once that they will not pass laws denying to black men the right to testify against white men in the courts of law.*[9]

As Douglass predicted, after Reconstruction, a long period of blatant discrimination followed in which blacks were socially segregated, lost their political power, were denied many civil rights, and at times were beaten and even killed. This terrible legacy of the Civil War lasted until the historic civil rights movements of the 1950s and 1960s, and the racism of that time lingers even today.

Not All Bad

Fortunately, some of the conflict's other legacies were more positive. By the end of 1865, the Freedmen's Bureau—the federal agency

PAST MEETS PRESENT: HERITAGE OR HATE?

An enduring controversy from the Civil War era centers around what is commonly called the Confederate flag, although it was never used as the official flag of the Confederacy, only as the battle flag of Robert E. Lee's troops. It later became the logo of Confederate veteran groups. Today, many people—especially people of color—see the flag as a symbol of hatred and slavery. Not only was it used during a war that sought to preserve the institution of slavery, it has since been used by many people in connection with violent crimes and hate speech against people of color. One notable example occurred in 2015, when a man named Dylann Roof shot and killed nine black people while they were attending a church service in Charleston, South Carolina. Roof had previously made posts online about his belief that white people were superior to people of color, accompanied by photos of himself posing with the Confederate flag. Because of this association of the flag with hatred, many stores have stopped selling items that have the Confederate flag design on them, and people have called for the removal of the flag from outside public buildings as well as for statues of Confederate leaders to be taken down from public spaces.

Others argue that the flag is a symbol of their heritage and that it honors the soldiers who fought for the Confederacy. Some of these people have relatives who fought in the war. However, historian John Coski pointed out that for years, "northern and African-American voices questioned the wisdom of displaying a flag they associated with disunity or treason. And young white southerners began using the flag in distinctly non-memorial ways as a symbol of regional identity."[1] Many people say that a symbol gets its meaning from the way the people using it behave. Someone who has a Confederate flag—either the flag itself or an item with the design, such as a bumper sticker or belt buckle—who also says or does racist things helps cement the association between the flag and racial hatred in other people's minds.

1. John Coski, "Myths & Misunderstandings: The Confederate Flag," American Civil War Museum, accessed October 29, 2019, acwm.org/blog/myths-misunderstandings-confederate-flag.

established to help freed slaves—had built 45 hospitals, enrolled 90,000 former slaves in school, and resettled some black people on available lands, among other accomplishments.

The Southern railroad lines destroyed in the war were quickly rebuilt. In addition, Northern lines underwent huge expansion both during and after the conflict, thanks in large part to two congressional acts passed in 1862 and 1864. These set in motion the creation of the first transcontinental railroad, completed in 1869. It proved instrumental in the remarkably rapid white settlement of the American West in the late 1800s.

The Civil War also generated huge advances in agriculture, partly because of new technology and inventions. At least half a million mechanical harvesters and mowers went into operation during the war. Millions more were purchased in the decades that followed, helping to transform the American Midwest into a gigantic breadbasket for both American and worldwide markets.

In the postwar years, the Civil War became a perpetual topic of interest and nostalgia for tens of thousands of historians and history fans. Thousands became reenactors, who still gather each year in authentic uniforms to restage some of the war's more famous battles.

The restoration of the Union also had positive effects on the country's standing in the world. Other countries recognized the United States as a nation that did not bend or hesitate under the test of its greatest threat yet. They were inspired by the North's victory, which many other countries saw as a triumph of democracy. In

1867, a statue of Lincoln was erected in London, England, in honor of his success at keeping the Union together, and France presented the United States with another statue—the Statue of Liberty—as a gift that symbolized that the two countries shared the same ideals.

Many people enjoy watching as well as participating in reenactments of some of the Civil War's most dramatic battles. Shown here are people reenacting the first day of the Battle of Gettysburg on its 150th anniversary.

However, the repercussions within the country's borders were much more complicated. Restoration should have meant brotherhood, but tensions between Northerners and Southerners remained high. It should have meant equality, but the institution of slavery was hard to bury. Although Reconstruction changed the economy of the South, it did not change opinions. Black people had to fight hard for the rights they had been promised; controversy over the rights of states versus the rights of the federal government still exists; and Confederate flags and statues are still prevalent. While other countries tend to try to move past their civil wars, the United States continues to celebrate and relive its civil war. With constant reminders of the conflict, it is no wonder tensions still exist within the country—and likely will for the foreseeable future.

How You See History

1. Do you think the South could have won the war? If so, how?
2. How would life be different today if the North had lost?
3. What lasting impacts do you think the Civil War has had on the United States?

TIMELINE

September 18, 1850

The US Congress enacts the Fugitive Slave Law, which allows federal agents to arrest runaway slaves anywhere in the country.

1852

Harriet Beecher Stowe publishes her novel *Uncle Tom's Cabin*, which strongly attacks the institution of slavery.

May 30, 1854

The Kansas-Nebraska Act allows the issue of slavery in the newly formed Kansas Territory to be decided by popular sovereignty, leading to the period known as Bleeding Kansas.

October 16, 1859

Abolitionist John Brown captures the US armory at Harpers Ferry, Virginia, causing outrage across the South.

November 6, 1860

Abraham Lincoln is elected president of the United States.

December 20, 1860

South Carolina is the first state to secede from the Union.

1861

Seven seceded states form the Confederate States of America; Confederate forces attack Fort Sumter, a US facility in South Carolina, marking the start of the Civil War; the Confederates score a victory at Bull Run in Virginia.

1862

Confederates defeat the Union in a second battle at Bull Run; Union forces win a narrow victory at Antietam in Maryland.

1863

Lincoln's Emancipation Proclamation legally ends slavery in the Confederacy; the Union wins major victories at Gettysburg, Pennsylvania, and Vicksburg, Mississippi; the all-black 54th Massachusetts Regiment fights bravely at Fort Wagner.

1864

Ulysses S. Grant becomes overall leader of Union forces; Atlanta falls to the Union army; Lincoln is reelected president.

1865

Confederate general Robert E. Lee surrenders his army at Appomattox Court House, Virginia; President Lincoln is assassinated by actor John Wilkes Booth; the Civil War officially ends on June 2 with the surrender of the Army of the Trans-Mississippi; the 13th Amendment abolishes slavery throughout the United States.

July 9, 1868

The 14th Amendment makes former slaves US citizens.

NOTES

Introduction: A Nation Divided

1. Quoted in Daniel Nasaw, "Who, What, Why: How Many Soldiers Died in the US Civil War?" BBC News, April 4, 2012, www.bbc.com/news/magazine-17604991.
2. "Jefferson Davis's Inaugural Address," Shotgun's Home of the American Civil War, modified November 21, 2004, www.civilwarhome.com/davisinauguraladdress.htm.

Chapter One: Heading Toward Conflict

1. Quoted in James M. McPherson, *Battle Cry of Freedom: The Civil War Era* (New York, NY: Oxford University Press, 2003), p. 100.
2. C.W. and A.J.K.D., "Did Slavery Make Economic Sense?," *Economist*, September 27, 2013, www.economist.com/free-exchange/2013/09/27/did-slavery-make-economic-sense.
3. Quoted in Michael Perman and Amy Murrell Taylor, eds., *Major Problems in the Civil War and Reconstruction* (Belmont, CA: Wadsworth, Cengage Learning, 2011), pp. 35–36.
4. Quoted in Perman and Taylor, *Major Problems in the Civil War and Reconstruction*, p. 31.
5. Quoted in Neil Kagan and Stephen G. Hyslop, *Eyewitness to the Civil War: The Complete History from Secession to Reconstruction* (Washington, DC: National Geographic, 2006), p. 26.
6. Quoted in Paul M. Angle, ed., *The Complete Lincoln-Douglas Debates of 1858* (Chicago, IL: University of Chicago Press, 1991), p. 60.
7. Quoted in Herbert Wender, *Southern Commercial Conventions, 1837–1859* (Baltimore, MD: Johns Hopkins University Press, 1930), p. 213.
8. "'House Divided' Speech by Abraham Lincoln," Abraham Lincoln Online, accessed December 2, 2019, www.abrahamlincolnonline.org/lincoln/speeches/house.htm.
9. Quoted in Stephen B. Oates, *To Purge the Land of Blood: A Biography of John Brown* (Amherst, MA: University of Massachusetts Press, 1984), p. 272.

Chapter Two: A Nation at War

1. George W. Nichols, *The Story of the Great March: From the Diary of a Staff Officer* (Bedford, MA: Applewood Books, 2008), p. 302.
2. Quoted in William E. Gienapp, "The Crime Against Sumner: The Caning of Charles Sumner and the Rise of the Republican Party," *Civil War History* 25, no. 3 (September 1979): p. 232.
3. Quoted in Gienapp, "The Crime Against Sumner," p. 222.
4. Quoted in Michael P. Johnson, *Toward a Patriarchal Republic: The Secession of Georgia* (Baton Rouge, LA: Louisiana State University Press, 1977), pp. 47–48.
5. Quoted in Howard C. Perkins, ed., *Northern Editorials on Secession* (New York, NY: Appleton-Century, 1942), p. 828.
6. Quoted in Richard N. Current, "Abraham Lincoln," *Encyclopædia Britannica*, modified October 4, 2019, www.britannica.com/biography/Abraham-Lincoln.
7. Quoted in Henry S. Commager, ed., *The Blue and the Gray: The Story of the Civil War As Told by Its Participants* (New York, NY: Fairfax Press, 1996), p. 47.
8. Quoted in Benjamin P. Thomas, *Abraham Lincoln: A Biography* (Carbondale, IL: Southern Illinois University Press, 2008), p. 268.
9. James M. McPherson, "Civil War," in Eric Foner and John A. Garraty, eds., *The Reader's Companion to American History* (Boston, MA: Houghton Mifflin, 1991), p. 186.

Chapter Three: 1863: A Pivotal Year

1. Quoted in "Letter to Horace Greeley," Abraham Lincoln Online, accessed December 2, 2019, www.abrahamlincolnonline.org/lincoln/speeches/greeley.htm.
2. Quoted in William H. Seward, "Transcript of the Proclamation," US National Archives, modified May 5, 2017, www.archives.gov/exhibits/featured-documents/emancipation-proclamation/transcript.html.
3. Quoted in William L. Katz, "January 1, 1863: When New Year's Day Meant Freedom," BlackPast.org, December 30, 2015, www.blackpast.org/african-american-history/january-1-1863-when-new-years-day-meant-freedom.
4. Rachel F. Seidman, ed., *The Civil War: A History in Documents* (New York, NY: Oxford University Press, 2001), pp. 133–34.

5. Quoted in Joseph Cummins, *History's Greatest Wars: The Epic Conflicts that Shaped the Modern World* (Beverly, MA: Fair Winds Press, 2011), p. 194.
6. Quoted in Ira Berlin et al., eds., *Free at Last: A Documentary History of Slavery, Freedom, and the Civil War* (New York, NY: New Press, 1992), p. 440.
7. Quoted in Henry S. Commager, ed., *The Blue and the Gray: The Story of the Civil War As Told by Its Participants* (New York, NY: Fairfax Press, 1996), p. 332.
8. Quoted in Sidney Kaplan, *American Studies in Black and White* (Amherst, MA: University of Massachusetts Press, 1991), p. 101.

Chapter Four: In the Field and at Home

1. Edward P. Alexander, *Military Memoirs of a Confederate* (New York, NY: Charles Scribner's Sons, 1907), p. 54.
2. Ian Drury and Tony Gibbons, *The Civil War Military Machine: Weapons and Tactics of the Union and Confederate Armed Forces* (New York, NY: Smithmark, 1993), p. 22.
3. Donald D. Jackson, *Twenty Million Yankees: The Northern Home Front* (New York, NY: Time-Life Books, 1985), p. 23.
4. Quoted in Steven A. Channing, *Confederate Ordeal: The Southern Home Front* (New York, NY: Time-Life Books, 1984), p. 17.
5. Quoted in Barbara M. Wertheimer, *We Were There: The Story of Working Women in America* (New York, NY: Pantheon Books, 1977), p. 143.
6. Quoted in Henry S. Commager, ed., *The Blue and the Gray: The Story of the Civil War As Told by Its Participants* (New York, NY: Fairfax Press, 1996), p. 786.
7. Quoted in Channing, *Confederate Ordeal*, p. 43.
8. Quoted in Jackson, *Twenty Million Yankees*, p. 102.

Chapter Five: The End of the Confederacy

1. Quoted in David J. Eicher, *The Longest Night* (New York, NY: Simon & Schuster, 2001), p. 723.
2. Quoted in David Colbert, ed., *Eyewitness to America: 500 Years of America in the Words of Those Who Saw It Happen* (New York, NY: Vintage Books, 1998), p. 272.

3. Quoted in Steven A. Channing, *Confederate Ordeal: The Southern Home Front* (New York, NY: Time-Life Books, 1984), p. 149.
4. Quoted in J. Matthew Gallman, ed., *The Civil War Chronicle: The Only Day-by-day Portrait of America's Tragic Conflict as Told by Soldiers, Journalists, Politicians, Farmers, Nurses, Slaves, and Other Eyewitnesses* (Bexley, OH: Gramercy Books, 2003), p. 517.
5. Quoted in James M. McPherson, *Battle Cry of Freedom: The Civil War Era* (New York, NY: Oxford University Press, 2003), p. 849.
6. Quoted in Eicher, *The Longest Night*, p. 820.
7. Quoted in Gallman, *The Civil War Chronicle*, p. 519.
8. Quoted in William Nester, *The Age of Lincoln and the Art of American Power, 1848–1876* (Lincoln, NE: Potomac Books, 2013), p. 200.
9. Frederick Douglass, "The Need for Continuing Anti-Slavery Work, speech at Thirty-Second Annual Meeting of the American Anti-Slavery Society, May 10, 1865," in Philip S. Foner and Yuval Taylor, eds., *Frederick Douglass: Selected Speeches and Writings* (Chicago, IL: Chicago Review Press, 2000), p. 578.

FOR MORE INFORMATION

Books: Nonfiction

Goodman, Michael E. *Civil War Spies*. Mankato, MN: Creative Education and Creative Paperbacks, 2016.

Hyslop, Stephen G. *Eyewitness to the Civil War*. Washington, DC: National Geographic, 2006.

Ohlin, Nancy, and Adam Larkum. *Blast Back!: The Civil War*. New York, NY: Little Bee Books, 2016.

Wright, John D. *50 Things You Should Know About the Civil War*. Lake Forest, CA: QEB, 2017.

Books: Fiction

Keith, Harold. *Rifles for Watie*. New York, NY: Harper Trophy, 1957.

Moss, Marissa. *A Soldier's Secret: The Incredible True Story of Sarah Edmonds, a Civil War Hero*. New York, NY: Amulet Books, 2012.

Nolen, Jerdine. *Calico Girl*. New York, NY: Simon & Schuster, 2017.

Websites

American Battlefield Trust: Civil War

www.battlefields.org/learn/civil-war

Take virtual tours of the battlefields, see past and present photos, and test your Civil War knowledge with quizzes and activities.

The Civil War: A Film by Ken Burns

www.pbs.org/civilwar

This website includes clips from Ken Burns's educational documentary about the war, as well as detailed maps and primary documents.

Civil War Timeline

www.nps.gov/gett/learn/historyculture/civil-war-timeline.htm

This informative timeline gives important dates from the Civil War, beginning with Abraham Lincoln's election and ending when the last Southern army surrendered in 1865.

The Music of the American Civil War

pdmusic.org/civilwar.html

This is an excellent collection of songs popularized in the North and South during the war.

Teaching with Documents: The Civil War as Photographed by Mathew Brady

www.archives.gov/education/lessons/brady-photos

This site displays several stunning photos taken by the most renowned of the Civil War photographers.

INDEX

PHOTO CREDITS

Cover, p. 82 Stock Montage/Stock Montage/Getty Images; pp. 4, 8, 34, 42, 59, 62, 72 Everett Historical/Shutterstock.com; p. 10, 78 Buyenlarge/Getty Images; pp. 15, 51, 67 Bettmann/Bettmann/Getty Images; pp. 19, 74 Courtesy of the Library of Congress; p. 21 Jon Bilous/Shutterstock.com; p. 24 StudioGShock/Shutterstock.com; p. 29 Mybona/Shutterstock.com; p. 32 DEA/Biblioteca Ambrosiana/De Agostini/Getty Images; p. 37 Photo12/Universal Images Group via Getty Images; p. 39 MPI/Getty Images; p. 40 The Print Collector/Getty Images; p. 47 KateShort/Shutterstock.com; p. 54 Jeffrey Greenberg/Universal Images Group via Getty Images; p. 56 Evan McCaffrey/Shutterstock.com; p. 63 Susan McAnnally/Shutterstock.com; p. 69 LMPC via Getty Images; p. 77 SSPL/Getty Images; p. 85 © CORBIS/Corbis via Getty Images; pp. 88–89 Nagel Photography/Shutterstock.com.

ABOUT THE AUTHOR

Donna Reynolds is a freelance writer and editor who has worked on more than 50 books for young adults. She has a degree in English from the University of Wisconsin—Madison and spends as much time as possible traveling around the world. She tries to volunteer at a local nonprofit organization at least one day a week, no matter where she happens to be.